The Friendship Book

A THOUGHT FOR EACH DAY | 2016

The Friendship Book

YESTERDAY has gone for ever,
Forget it, let it go,
Look forward with a happy heart,
Tomorrow's yours, you know.

The future is an open gate
With pathways leading on,
And there's a bright horizon now
The troubled past is gone.

Tomorrow's just a dream away,
So make that dream come true,
With flag unfurled take on the world,
Tomorrow is for you!

– Iris Hesselden.

January

Friday — January 1

AS we start another year, we all tend to wonder what it will hold. Sometimes we are glad to leave the old year behind us, to forget its worries and its problems, and to set out hopefully on a new journey.

The last year, of course, had its highlights and happy times and left us with some pleasant memories. Perhaps we are not quite so eager to dismiss them.

However, we need to move forward and these delightful words by T.S. Eliot sum it all up so well:

"For last year's words belong to last year's language and next year's words await another voice. And to make an end is to make a beginning."

If there has been some kind of ending in your life, perhaps now is the time for a new beginning.

I hope it will be a successful one for you, and a year of peace and goodwill for us all.

Saturday — January 2

WHAT are the most important aspects of any journey? Booking your tickets? Packing a good lunch? Getting plenty of leg-room?

The gospel singer Gloria Gaither thought there were two things worth remembering.

"We may run, walk, stumble, drive, or fly," she said, "but let us never lose sight of the reason for the journey – or miss a chance to see a rainbow on the way."

Good advice for every kind of travelling, be it a day-trip or the grander journey that is life!

Sunday — January 3

*R*EMEMBER to spotlight the good things
When times appear troubled or grey,
When the briefest of heartening moments
Can bring happiness to your day.

A kiss or a hug from a loved one;
A smile from a stranger you passed,
A quick heart-to-heart with an old friend,
A chore you've completed at last.

So, if there are moments of gladness,
No matter how fleeting or slight,
Turn the spotlight on that which is pleasing,
And dark days may come to be bright.

– Emma Canning.

Monday — January 4

I CAME across some words recently that really struck a chord with me, and I would like to share them with you. This is something said to that wonderful writer, Catherine Cookson, whilst she was still a young girl.

They must have made an impression on her, as she remembered them many years later.

"Have one aim in life – happiness! If you are happy you'll make at least half the people you know happy."

At first glance, aiming for happiness might sound like rather a selfish thing to do. However, I'm sure we all have discovered that sharing laughter and joy with others creates ripples of happiness which spread far and wide.

Sometimes we find that even a small act of kindness can set off a surprisingly wide circle of ripples, spreading all sorts of goodwill in all sorts of unexpected quarters!

In this tired, troubled world of ours, we should all "aim for happiness", but most of all, we should try to make others happy, too. And I'm sure you will agree.

Tuesday — January 5

Do you have a method for your life?

Most people know John Wesley helped found the Methodist movement, but fewer folk know where the name Methodism came from.

While at university Wesley and friends decided to try to live holier lives. To help, they kept notes of their feelings, their behaviour, their works, often on an hourly basis. By doing this they could identify strengths and shortcomings, then work on them. They improved their lives, and their service to God, methodically.

Want to improve your spirituality, your patience, your . . . whatever? Buy a notepad – and get yourself a method!

Wednesday — January 6

THE Dalai Lama was once asked what surprised him most about humanity. His reply was, "Man, who sacrifices his health to make money, then sacrifices his money to recover his health." If you have your health, you have your wealth, as the wise old saying goes, and this is as true today as it ever was. Appreciate good health, and nurture it.

Thursday — January 7

I STARTLED four young deer on my morning walk. Then I watched in awe as they took to the air (or so it seemed), covering half a mile in a series of graceful bounds. It all seemed to take no more than a few seconds.

The moorland was covered with dense undergrowth that I would have struggled to walk through. So how was it that the deer travelled so effortlessly? Could it be because they spent so much time in the air? And I wondered how far and how quickly I might travel if I spent less time tangled in the undergrowth of life; the trivial, the negative, the hurtful.

Will you join me in being more like those deer, unencumbered by the low-lying stuff and striving always for the higher way?

Friday — January 8

WE recently heard this little story and found it extremely heartwarming.

An elderly couple had cause to be taken to hospital late at night. Fortunately it turned out not to be too serious, but the gentleman was kept in overnight for observation.

His wife made her way to the exit, where she realised she had only a few coins in her purse. Certainly not sufficient for a taxi ride home.

As she pondered on what to do, a younger couple appeared beside her, also on their way out. They enquired what the problem was. On hearing the lady's plight, the younger woman took out her wallet and handed her a £10 note.

The older lady asked for an address so she could return it. However, the answer was "Please accept it. Some day someone will help me when I am in need."

There are still Good Samaritans around. Who knows when and where we might meet them?

Or could they be angels in disguise?

Saturday — January 9

AS Karen would be first to agree, she is a perfectionist. It can be an admirable trait in many ways, but perhaps not if applied too rigorously.

She smiled ruefully as she admitted that, without meaning to, she'd gradually found herself applying unreasonably high standards to those around her.

"But I was lucky," she continued. "I recently made a mess of some party arrangements, and my friends were so forgiving that it made me wonder just how I myself would have behaved. Now I treat others a little more kindly!"

Whatever the relationship, I like these words from the philosopher Sam Keen, who said, "We come to love not by finding a perfect person, but by learning to see an imperfect person perfectly."

Sounds good to me!

Sunday — January 10

TIME to talk with God? Where can we find that in the hectic schedule of the modern world? Well, you might sympathise with this unnamed mother from a generation when families were large and labour-saving devices were few. The only way she could take herself away from it all for a moment, it seems, was by throwing her pinny over her head.

She wrote:

"I shuts my eyes
As I sits in my chair
It's up with my apron
And I'm at prayer."

How silly must she have looked? Can you picture God laughing? If He did I am sure it would be through sheer delight that the hard-worked soul didn't mind looking foolish to find a place where they could meet!

Now, where can we find a few moments to share with Him?

Monday — January 11

PROVERBS from other countries have always interested me. For instance, I came across this one from Ethiopia: "When spiders' webs unite, they can tie up a lion". We won't be tying up any lions here, but we can stop to think how much strength there is in numbers, wherever you live. We needn't tackle onerous tasks alone if friends can help us accomplish them.

Tuesday — January 12

WHATEVER you can do, or dream you can do, begin it. Boldness has genius, power and magic in it. Begin it now." This observation was originally attributed to Goethe, but research traced it to W.H. Murray, a Scots explorer and writer who tackled the Himalayas. Murray achieved his pinnacle of success with his boldness – why don't you, starting now?

Safe Harbour

Wednesday — January 13

DO you sometimes feel there are compensations for growing older?

If we can put aside any aches and pains or discomfort, we discover a new kind of freedom. We no longer have to rush from place to place. Time is not the stern master it used to be, and we can really be ourselves.

Writer Elizabeth Coatsworth must have made the same discovery. She said, "During much of my life, I was anxious to be what someone else wanted me to be. Now I have given up that struggle. I am what I am."

Maybe we would all be happier had we learned that lesson at an earlier age!

Thursday — January 14

OUR old friend Molly took a tumble in her flat.

Unfortunately her wrist was broken, but after X-rays and with her arm in plaster, she was allowed home.

In spite of the discomfort and the frustration, she remained remarkably cheerful. The first time we took her shopping, she seemed quite amused by people's reactions.

"Have you noticed," she asked us, "how the other shoppers all smile at me sympathetically?"

We hadn't realised, but of course she was right. One rather tall man, with his arm in a bright blue sling, grinned at Molly in a very friendly fashion. I felt he would have enjoyed discussing their injuries had there been sufficient time!

Later in the day, when Molly was safely settled in her armchair and we had returned home, I thought about her words.

Why, I wondered, can't we all smile at each other every day? Perhaps in a shopping mall or supermarket we could all use a little smile.

What do you think? Shall we give it a try?

Friday — January 15

EDDIE was telling me of his experience of running a village youth club.

"It started very promisingly," he said. "The kids were enthusiastic and everyone worked well together. Then, within the space of a few weeks, several of our keenest members left to go to university; we had a flood on the premises, and no-one seemed interested in helping put it right. I have to admit, I was almost ready to give up when a couple of youngsters arrived with brushes and cleaning materials all ready to do what they could." He laughed.

"They couldn't possibly have done it on their own, but their attitude completely changed my own. And once that happened, more and more people came forward to volunteer."

It was Albert Schweitzer who said, "Sometimes our light goes out, but is blown again into instant flame by an encounter with another human being."

How true – and how wonderful to be the sort of person who helps reignite the fire.

Saturday — January 16

NO doubt the sun dial was a pretty thing, but Mary seemed more than usually engrossed with it. Pointing to the narrow triangular shadow cast on the stone, she asked me, "What does that tell you, Francis?"

"Well," I said, preparing to show my wisdom, "its position between those two Latin numerals tells me it is approximately twenty-eight minutes past one in the afternoon. What does it tell you?"

She drew an arc with her finger, from one side of the dark shape, all the way around the dial to the other side.

"It tells me that where there is shadow, there is always much more light."

I was right about the time on the sun dial, I consoled myself, but, on another level, the real time was time I started seeing things the way dear old Mary does!

Sunday — January 17

IT'S often at this time of year that people start looking ahead and planning their summer holiday. I have seen lots of tips for travellers, but here are a few extra ones for the longer journey that we all take:

"Focus on the journey, not the destination. Joy is found not in finishing an activity but in doing it." Greg Anderson.

"It's funny how, in this journey of life, even though we may begin at different times and places, our paths cross with others so that we may share our love, compassion, observations and hope." Steve Maraboli.

And, most helpful of all: "It doesn't matter how slow you go, as long as you don't stop." Confucius.

Monday — January 18

DON'T worry about the world coming to an end today. It's already tomorrow in Australia."

Reading that remark from the "Peanuts" cartoonist Charles M. Schulz at first made me laugh, but secondly made me think. How often we do fret about dark clouds on the horizon that blow away long before they reach us? Next time I start to lose sleep over thoughts of things that might never happen, I shall remember that a bright tomorrow is almost certainly on its way!

Tuesday — January 19

SCIENCE, my lad, is made up of mistakes, but they are mistakes which it is useful to make, because they lead little by little to the truth."

Well, I'm not quite sure who Jules Verne was addressing when he spoke those words, but I do know that they shouldn't just be restricted to the discipline of science.

No-one likes getting things wrong, but one thing is certain. There is no more effective teacher than a mistake, and no more certain route to success than learning from it.

Wednesday — January 20

HOW would you like to visit paradise? It's my guess that many of us already have. We only have to work on realising it and appreciating it.

Country singer Johnny Cash knew the secret of getting there. When asked in an interview what his definition of paradise was, he pointed to June, his wife of thirty-five years, and said, "This morning . . . with her . . . having coffee."

Paradise – it might be closer than you think!

Thursday — January 21

IT'S easily done, when a failing's our own,
To think disapprovingly, "I should have known!"
"I should have done better." "How foolish of me."
And judge it with harshness, not leniency.

Yet, if a companion were in such a plight,
What kind of response would we deem to be right?
To chide in a stern and intolerant fashion,
Or speak words of tenderness, care and compassion?

Perhaps, "No-one's perfect" or "You tried your best,"
And words of encouragement, kindly expressed,
So next time you don't quite accomplish perfection,
Treat yourself as you would treat your friends – with affection!
– Emma Canning.

Friday — January 22

IF today someone asks you, "How are you?" you might reply, "Not bad" or perhaps "Fair to middling" or "Oh, OK, I suppose". These answers indicate that your mind is in a downbeat mood. Therefore, by answering in another way, like "Fantastic, thanks!" or "Terrific!" or "Wonderful!" your mind will focus on the upbeat, and you'll feel more energised. Try it and let it become a habit.

Saturday — January 23

A VIOLIN – or is it a vile din? John was laughing as he assured me that his parents would have definitely plumped for the latter definition – at least while he was a child learning how to play.

"Nevertheless," he continued, "it didn't stop them giving me their full support. However painful my efforts, they always supported me, and helped me to see that my practising was achieving results."

Today John is a well-respected musician whose favoured instrument certainly doesn't make a vile din.

Which just goes to show, I think, how a little encouragement at the right time can really help us all create something worth listening to.

Sunday — January 24

*A T the edge of the morning
The fringe of the night,
Our dreams fade like mist
With the coming of light.
And thoughts gather round
As the world closes in,
Another day starting,
A time to begin.
At the edge of the morning
As night slips away,
Be hopeful and cheerful
And welcome today!*

– Iris Hesselden.

Monday — January 25

W HEN you awoke this morning, did you feel lucky?
Well, scientists believe there is no such thing as luck. People either expect good or bad things to happen to them and that reflects in their expectations of life. If you expect good things, you're the optimist, the "Lucky" one.

So be lucky: start expecting the good things this very day!

Tuesday — January 26

THERE'S bound to be more to it than I know. Perhaps it's an eastern philosophy, or a school of art, or something to do with fashion, but when I heard that "shibui" was Japanese for the appreciation and practice of simple, subtle and unobtrusive beauty I thought of one person straight away.

Who does it call to your mind? And wouldn't it be wonderful to have others think of us as shibui?

Maybe it was you I thought of!

Wednesday — January 27

IF you think, "How will I manage
One day when far from home?"
Or, "How long the days and nights will be
When I'm left all alone."

Don't let your limitations
Ever weaken your resolve,
There are always ways to overcome
Those problems we can't solve.

We may have means to save a life
Not known to us at all;
So stop and wait. Be ready
To take that higher call.

– Dawn Lawrence.

Thursday — January 28

WHILE passing some time in the calm of a churchyard, I saw an inscription on the gravestone of a local man. It read, "I was old, with many problems. Most did not materialise."

Those wise words really gave me pause for thought.

I hope the gentleman has found peace in the afterlife.

Friday — January 29

I **AM** sure Joan won't mind me revealing that she recently celebrated her ninetieth birthday, for she is rightly proud of that achievement.

But she smiled as she told me of how, when she reached her fifties, she had assumed she'd be unlikely to learn any new skills.

"Then I read some words of Henri Frederic Amiel." She chuckled. "He said, 'How to grow old is the master work of wisdom and one of the most difficult chapters in the great art of living.' Since then, I've done my best to get to grips with it."

Well, looking at Joan, I think she's a star pupil!

Saturday — January 30

THERE are three things you can do today to help you take stock of your life and face up to whatever challenges are presented to you.

1. Think back with thankfulness for the life you have enjoyed.
2. Think forward with hope in your heart.
3. Look heavenward and feel the self-confidence within you.

Sunday — January 31

SOMETIMES we can be so focused upon what we think we need, that we forget to consider that there may be other solutions that would actually be better for us."

Those words were uttered by Marianne, who was telling me about a particularly difficult year that she'd been through. Happily, although the closure of her business had initially hit her hard, it had also allowed her to discover a talent for design which is now taking her in whole new and exciting directions.

It was John H. Groberg who observed that, "We should always pray for help. But we should always listen for inspiration and impression to proceed in ways different from those we may have thought of."

Something to remember next time we feel our prayers aren't being answered.

Wrap Up Warm!

February

Monday — February 1

IT was a "flash mob" in a Spanish plaza. A little girl stepped up to a busker and gave him a coin. In response he started playing the hymn "Joyful, Joyful".

Another musician stepped from the crowd and stood by the first. Then another, and another, all keeping time with the music. Before long there was a full orchestra playing in the square.

It was set up to be filmed, of course, and it spread across the internet because it was so different. But I believe something similar happens somewhere every day. Perhaps many times a day.

Each time someone reaches out to help a brother or sister in need I am convinced a choir of angels steps forward, unseen but still there, and sings a joyful song!

Tuesday — February 2

ARE you in touch with your creative side? Studies have shown that creative folk are healthier folk: fewer GP visits, fewer prescription or medical needs. They have a better quality of life because they are more socially active, more outgoing, with good friends. Their self-esteem is enhanced as a result. And it is a basic human need to create. All it takes for you to benefit is to do something, make something, or simply get out and be sociable. Create a new acquaintance this very day!

Wednesday — February 3

A FARMER friend of mine told me that he often stopped to watch his cattle lazing around chewing the cud. They always seem at total peace with themselves and their calmness transfers to him, he said. They have not a care in the world and, for a time thereafter, neither does he! I'm going to try it next time I see a field of cows!

Thursday — February 4

I *WELL* recall – though long gone by – how, in my childhood years,
My bedroom, in the gloom of night, seemed full of nameless fears.
The china pig, the music box, the gown behind the door,
In darkness took on different forms, too scary to ignore.
It wasn't till, as time slipped by, and understanding grew,
I saw my fears for what they were – illusions, quite untrue.
And as an adult, now I find that lesson's served me well.
It's taught me all that looms unknown, does not disaster spell,
For even though I may not know what's hid beyond my sight,
Yet still I see no shadow can defeat the Greater Light.

– Margaret Ingall.

Friday — February 5

W ALKING along the beach the other day, enjoying the fresh
sea air, I chuckled to myself as I watched a Great Dane and a
tiny little terrier go nose to nose as if saying hello to each other – or
perhaps wondering if the other, so different, was the same species!

What was just as fascinating, however, was the other walkers'
reactions. We'd each been absorbed in our own thoughts,
preoccupied and not really getting the most out of the lovely day.
But suddenly smiles broke out, amused looks were exchanged.

Shoulders became less bowed, foreheads cleared, and the warmth
of that little friendly exchange between two dogs seemed to reach
out to envelop every one of us.

Saturday — February 6

A RT students have many teachers. They have their lecturers and
they have every artist they ever studied to learn from. But
my young friend added one more to the list, explaining that her
grandmother taught her the most important lesson about drawing.

"She taught me that even a scribble on a page can be turned into a
tree, or the wind, or a flock of birds – if you just look at it right."

Now, I think Gran may have been teaching her granddaughter
about more than just art with that advice – if I'm looking at it right.

Sunday — February 7

DO you know the hymn "Beyond The Sunset"? The story behind it is well worth sharing. One evening in 1936, a group of friends described a sunset over Winona Lake in Indiana to their blind companion, Horace Burr, and his reply made them all pause.

"I see through other people's eyes, and I think I often see more – I see beyond the sunset."

Amongst the party was his cousin Virgil Brock and his wife, and later all three got together to write a hymn inspired by the incident.

"Beyond the sunset, a hand will guide me
To God the Father whom I adore.
His glorious presence, His words of welcome,
Will be my portion on that fair shore."

I think those words deserve to be sung more often, don't you?

Monday — February 8

THE author Jessica Markwell recalled childhood years spent in a farmhouse without mains power. Most evenings her father would crank up the generator and they would have half an hour of electricity. When the lights came on Jessica and her sister would already be sitting there with their books open, determined not to miss a minute of precious reading time.

Opportunities for enjoyment or advancement in this life might be few or frequent, but if we want to make the most of them we ought to follow the example of those two keen young readers – and be prepared!

Tuesday — February 9

AN acquaintance who has no pets of her own was asked to dog-sit while a relative went on holiday. What our friend discovered for the first time in her life, she told the Lady of the House, was how the dog's trust, faithfulness and affection began to banish any fears or doubts she was feeling within herself. A joyful revelation, indeed. To have a faithful pet is to have a great gift in life.

Still Waters

Wednesday — February 10

LIKE my garden. I like my books. I like reading a book in the garden. But I never really saw much of a connection between the two until I heard the old Chinese saying, "A book is a garden you can carry about in your pocket."

I can only imagine they meant that beautiful flowers blossom in a garden and beautiful ideas can blossom in books. So, if ever the hang of my jacket seems a little off – if there seems to be a rectangular object pulling it out of shape – just assume I'm doing a little gardening!

Thursday — February 11

IF you feel that you are struggling,
And your daily trials grown,
Don't fear to hold a hand out –
Look around, you're not alone.
There are those who long to help you,
Who are happy to give aid,
Don't be too proud to let them,
Too reserved or too afraid.
For giving and accepting
Are both blessed in equal part
And neither could exist without
An open, loving heart.

– Margaret Ingall.

Friday — February 12

AGED fifty-one and feeling really ill, John Wesley wrote his own epitaph. It was short and the main thrust of it was that, after paying his debts, he would only have ten pounds to leave behind. He described himself as "unprofitable".

Thirty-five years later Wesley went to meet his beloved Saviour, leaving behind a life that has inspired generations. The moral of this? Never write yourself off just because the going gets tough. God can turn a profit from your life in the most unexpected ways.

Saturday — February 13

TWO hungry travellers met by a cherry tree. Seeing there weren't many cherries on the branches, one man grabbed as many as he could, eating as he gathered. The other man took a single cherry, looked at it from every angle, smelled it, then sat down on the grass and slowly ate it.

He rose afterwards feeling he had tasted every cherry, while the other man (who would have eaten every cherry if he could) walked off with a tummy ache.

It's so often the case that in settling for less, we actually gain so much more.

Sunday — February 14

ST VALENTINE'S DAY is all about love! So here is a wise observation from Winnie-the-Pooh.

"Some people care too much. I think it's called love."

I'm not sure you can care too much for someone, but it's a delightful sentiment, isn't it?

Monday — February 15

THE Lady of the House was delighted with the small fridge magnet. It had a beautiful picture of a rainbow, but it was the words which really appealed to her.

"Look at this, Francis," she said, "the words we so often say to each other and to other people, too."

The words were *Carpe Diem* and, as you know, they mean "Seize the day."

As we grow older and time passes quickly, it seems to me that it becomes more important really to value each and every day and to make the most of it.

This tiny gift now has pride of place on the fridge door and on dark days, the rainbow, too, is a vision of hope.

Tuesday — February 16

NOW, here's a challenge. Close your eyes for a moment and describe aloud the sort of person that comes to mind when you think of a hero. Did I hear the words "big", "strong" or "bold" near the top of the list?

I have to confess that I'd probably have been among that chorus, but a thought from Pam Brown has made me think a little harder. She said, "The courage of very ordinary people is all that stands between us and the dark."

Very ordinary people. Not some special race marked out by destiny, but folk like you and me who find themselves faced with a challenge – and rise to it.

An inspiring thought, don't you agree?

Wednesday — February 17

THOSE we care for never leave us,
Even when our ways must part,
All the things that made them special
Live for ever in our heart.
There in precious sweet reflection,
Safe from harm, we hold them near,
Loved and loving still we feel them,
Ever close and ever dear.

– Margaret Ingall.

Thursday — February 18

HERE is a short verse I chanced upon, penned by English writer and poet Frederick Langbridge: "Two men look through the same prison bars. One sees mud, the other stars."

I took a moment to ponder this in terms of happiness. Are you blessed with a positive outlook? Most of the time you can choose your own attitude to life. I'm going to make a point of remembering that in future . . .

Friday — February 19

DECIDING how best to respond to people who are unkind or unpleasant isn't always easy. But neither was understanding my dear friend Mary's advice on the subject!

"Remember they probably have a mirror at home," she told me.

My normally befuddled expression must have reached new extremes of confusion because Mary laughed and took pity on me.

"By that I mean they don't need you to be their reflection! Show them something different."

So, I showed Mary something different. I showed her my dawning understanding!

Saturday — February 20

I HEARD a song on the radio recently which asked, "What have you done today to make you feel proud?"

That single line made me question myself. What had I done that day to make myself feel proud? Had I done my good deed for the day yet?

Have you?

Sunday — February 21

THE message on the window of the chapel was written in large letters and was very eye catching. Only two words, but such powerful words: *Prayer Works*.

It almost stopped me in my tracks and certainly made an impression. As I continued on my way, I thought about this a great deal. I remembered many occasions when prayer had been so important.

Times when friends and loved ones had been ill or in need of help. Times when people in hospital had been aware of healing thoughts sent out to them and prayers being said.

Quite suddenly I felt uplifted and my steps seemed lighter. Yes, I decided, it is true! Prayer really does work!

OLD age doesn't have to be the demon most people seem to think. Recently we have been encouraged by hearing of several "mature persons" who, though by no means as active as they once were, still thoroughly enjoy their lives.

One in particular is a gentleman of one hundred and one who attends Salvation Army services and still lives alone – albeit with a little help from family and friends.

Another is a lady we meet when out shopping. She is tall and slim and quite sprightly and we were surprised to learn she is eighty. She greeted us today with the words, "What a beautiful morning, and how lovely to see a blue sky."

She was right, of course, but not everyone seemed to appreciate it.

I was reminded of these words by Thomas Bailey Aldrich:

"To keep the heart unwrinkled, to be hopeful, kindly, cheerful, reverent – that is to triumph over old age."

I hope that we all will be equally triumphant!

DOROTHY was looking very cheerful when I bumped into her, so I was surprised when she confided that she'd come from a dentist's appointment.

"I've just finished the last of a course of treatment," she said. "I'm really thrilled it's over, because at first I was so nervous that I nearly backed out of having it done at all. It's silly, I know, but now I'm feeling quite proud of myself."

Silly? I don't think so. Everyone has their own particular fears in life, whether others deem them reasonable or not.

It was Eleanor Roosevelt who said these wise words: "You gain strength, courage and confidence by every experience in which you really stop to look fear in the face. You must do the thing which you think you cannot do."

And if you can achieve that – yes, be proud, for you have every reason to be!

Wednesday — February 24

THE German language has the dubious distinction of including a word for taking pleasure in someone else's misfortune – *schadenfreude*. How sad. There really ought to be an opposite word. Well, you might have to go to India to find it but there is one!

Mudita is the Sanskrit word for taking pleasure in the good fortune of others, even if there's nothing in it for you. What a wonderful concept!

Neither of those words is likely to crop up in our everyday spoken language. But one or the other is bound to feature in the language of our heart . . .

Thursday — February 25

YOU'VE heard of sticks and carrots
As methods to persuade?
The carrot to encourage,
The stick to make afraid.
Such methods make me wonder
Why sticks are ever used,
For what could be productive
When power is misused?
So should you be the person
Who fills the driver's seat,
Make sure you just use carrots –
You'll travel far and fleet!

– Margaret Ingall.

Friday — February 26

SUSAN absolutely hates to be late. Her younger sister, though, is the complete opposite – and it frequently drives Susan mad!

One day, when her sister was running almost half an hour late for a family gathering, Susan voiced her frustration to her great-aunt. That wise lady suggested a different point of view, as counselled by Winnie-the-Pooh author A.A. Milne: "Rivers know this: there is no hurry. We shall get there some day."

Tumbling Down

Saturday — February 27

THE checkout operator asked the man how he was doing.

"Oh," he said, barely lifting his head from the bags he was packing. "Getting there . . . getting there." Then he stopped, considered, then added, "We say that, don't we? 'I'm getting there.' But where are we getting to, I wonder?"

There were three of us there, probably with three different ideas on the subject. But given that we pass this way only once I would suggest it's a question worth thinking about.

Choose a destination; choose a purpose. And I hope you choose one that is well worth spending a lifetime "getting there."

Sunday — February 28

FRIENDS were talking about the days of "make do and mend" when people didn't just throw things away. Out would come the work-box, and a bed-sheet that had worn thin in the middle would be cut in half. The two outer edges were sewn together and the worn parts (now on the outer edges) were tucked under the mattress.

It occurred to me that those worn-out things were given new leases of life; they became useful again. Now, if only we could do that with people!

We can't – but God can. He has a work-box big enough and I know He hates to throw anything away. But, maybe we could help unpick someone from the life they are in, and give a hand turning them around for Him.

Monday — February 29

THIS is the day on which a lady may ask her gentleman friend for his hand in marriage. A young friend of the Lady of the House confided to her that she was going to propose to her boyfriend by means of a verse she had read in a greetings card.

"The sun will rise, the day will pass, then night must fall. I have no fears; my love for you will conquer all."

What a lovely sentiment – I can't wait to hear how it turns out!

March

Tuesday — March 1

HOLLYWOOD star Elizabeth Taylor lived an incredibly glamorous life. She had everything anyone could ever ask for – but did she ever find happiness?

In one interview she suggested she had. And she did it in a way you don't need to be rich and famous to try.

"I don't go out looking for affirmation any longer," she said. "Instead I go out and affirm other people. I tell other people I love them and I'm glad they're alive. I don't look for fulfilment, I look for ways I can fulfil others. And I found happiness that way."

Wednesday — March 2

I'VE always been a believer in the general excellence of flowers, but was pleased to have my view even more firmly reinforced when I began reading about the Orchid Project of Writhlington School at Radstock.

This began more than 20 years ago, when the after-school Gardening Club was given a small collection of orchids. A trivial beginning, but one which, under the direction of teacher Simon Pugh-Jones, grew amazingly.

Since then hundreds of students have been involved with growing, studying, selling and exhibiting them, even winning medals at the RHS Chelsea Flower Show.

But perhaps the biggest success of this project has been the way it's engaged the enthusiasm of students who might otherwise have given up on education.

The Orchid Project has opened avenues of interest to even the most disenfranchised of students, and the result is that the whole school has blossomed.

An achievement just as impressive as a medal!

SOMETHING to look forward to
However small that seems,
A goal or an ambition,
Some special hopes and dreams.
A little gift to please a friend
And give them a surprise,
Don't miss an opportunity
As time so quickly flies.

Watch the sunset, count the stars
And count your blessings, too,
And in the busy whirl of life
Take time for being you.
Something to look forward to:
The coming of the spring,
Music, laughter, hope and love,
The joy of everything!

So as the road goes winding on,
Step bravely, mile by mile,
Through sun and showers, hope and joy,
The journey is worthwhile!

– Iris Hesselden.

HOW do you measure the health of someone's body? Well, doctors have countless ways of doing it, and I'm sure you know them all; they might measure the degree of agility, the capacity of the lungs, the percentage of weight given over to fat, or the level of sugars in the blood.

How do you measure the health of someone's personality? According to Ralph Waldo Emerson, you don't need any medical training at all to do that. Each person's personality, he explained, was healthy "to the exact degree to which they have the propensity to look for the good in every situation."

Saturday — March 5

A LICE HERTZ-SOMMER passed away in 2014, aged one hundred and nine. The previous year she was asked the secret of her long life and she insisted it was optimism.

She said, "Everything is a gift" and "I look where it is good. I know about the bad, but I look at the good things." Lovely sentiments but a little simplistic, perhaps?

Oh, did I mention Alice was the oldest survivor of the Nazi concentration camps?

Optimism might be more powerful than most people realise!

Sunday — March 6

I F you attended the "Moleskin Church" in Glasgow in the late 1800s you had to pass inspection at the door. Rev. Dr Norman Macleod had heard that many working folk didn't come to church because they lacked suits and hats and the like.

So, he made it a rule that everyone should wear their working clothes to the services. (Moleskin being favoured by working men.) Church elders turned away anyone who was too well dressed!

The services were phenomenally successful. Many "high-heid yins" wanted to hear the sermons but were turned away on account of finery that would have seen them welcomed at great cathedrals.

If we want to join in the worship up above, there will also be a selection of sorts. Expensive clothes won't see you through. Neither, indeed, will working clothes, unless they are worn out in works of love. That inspection committee will be looking deeper than the skin – to the humility of the heart!

Monday — March 7

F RIENDS who recently moved house received a New Home card whose message was an Irish blessing: "May the roof above you never fall in, and may those living beneath it never fall out". What a lovely wish for harmony in their new abode, don't you think?

Tuesday — March 8

JIM used to be an impatient sort of fellow; the kind of man who didn't suffer fools gladly. I had just seen him in a situation where he might have lost his temper – but didn't! So I asked what made the difference.

If someone annoyed him these days, Jim told me, he reminded himself of some truths – "Just like me, this person is looking for happiness from life. Just like me, this person is trying to avoid suffering. Just like me, this person has known sadness. Just like me, this person is trying to fulfil his needs. And, just like me, this person is learning the rules of life as he goes along."

Being cross with anyone was impossible after that. A friend had told him these truths and Jim had been very impressed – just like me!

Wednesday — March 9

I'VE heard it asked several times. "What three words of advice would you give if you could talk to your younger self?"

Inevitably, some people have a laugh. But, of the people who take it seriously, the vast majority choose to send words of love and encouragement.

Now, it's just a game and of course it's impossible to send messages back in time. But do you know what is possible? We can send those messages of support and affirmation to our present selves, and benefit from them in the here and now.

Thursday — March 10

IN quiet conversation the Lady of the House told me that she had overheard a mother trying to comfort her teenage daughter who had broken up with her boyfriend.

"The only way out of emotional upset is to travel through it," she counselled her daughter.

We decided that girl was bound to be all right when she had such a wise parent to lean on.

Friday — March 11

HOW do you make the world a better place from your armchair?

Tinney Davidson and her husband weren't really fit enough to get out and about, but their living-room window looked on to a road leading to a high school. So they started waving to the students as they passed by.

Her husband eventually passed on, but Tinney kept up what was by now a tradition, waving to students on their way to school and on their way home.

The students waved back, but she had no idea the difference she was making to their lives until they invited her to a school assembly.

The assembly had been called for one sole purpose – to say thank you to Tinney for lifting their spirits day after day, and year after year!

How do you change the word from your armchair, or wherever you might be? Even if you have nothing else to work with, a smile and a friendly wave will do!

Saturday — March 12

*A*N ordinary day, an ordinary street
But nature has a magic all her own,
She touches hedges with a silver frost
And traces patterns on the bricks and stone.

An ordinary morning, dull and grey,
But see, the signs of spring are all around,
And soon the earth will wake with joy and beauty
As we rejoice, with every sight and sound.

An ordinary week, what does it hold?
Will there be happy times for me and you?
For nature gives us sunshine after shadow
And life is extraordinary, too!

– Iris Hesselden.

Sunday — March 13

IN the churchyard last Sunday, I noticed that one of our parishioners was sitting on a bench, deeply immersed in his Bible, reading and then staring skyward, then reading again and staring upwards again.

He noticed my quizzical expression and said to me, "Reading the Bible without reflecting upon it is like eating without chewing, or drinking without tasting."

I would agree – wouldn't you?

Monday — March 14

WOULD you like to see a beautiful work of art?
There is a 12-feet-high ornamental picture frame in Long Bay Regional Park in New Zealand. What does it frame? Nothing – except for a view of the park and the bay.

I am sure people would have enjoyed the view anyway, but putting a frame there to view it through somehow focuses the attention and helps visitors enjoy the scenery all the more.

So if you want to see a work of art, step out into this beautiful world of ours and, wherever you look, frame it with appreciation.

Tuesday — March 15

I HADN'T seen Graham for a while, so I was pleased to hear that he'd been enjoying a visit from his nephew Steve who lives in California.

"It was good to see him," Graham confided, "for he was involved in a car accident a while ago, from which he's only just recovering. And he told me that his enforced career-break had allowed him time to take his first steps as a professional writer – which he's finding to be enormously rewarding." He chuckled.

"It seems he was inspired by some words of Jon Kabat-Zinn, who's a Mindfulness teacher and Professor of Medicine. He said, 'You can't stop the waves, but you can learn to surf'."

I suspect life is always full of possibilities for those who choose to think positive.

A Fine Day Out!

Wednesday — March 16

HAVE you ever wished to own a magic carpet?

I suspect I'm not alone in having sometimes thought how wonderful such a thing would be – just before I descend to earth with a bump with the depressing recollection that they don't actually exist!

Or do they? For some words of American novelist Caroline Gordon have made me think again.

She said, "A well-composed book is a magic carpet on which we are wafted to a world that we cannot enter in any other way."

An excellent observation, for a good book can indeed give us access to an unlimited universe. And without even needing to hang on tightly!

Thursday — March 17

IF the day seems turbulent,
Or anxious thoughts intrude,
Sit a while and contemplate
In quiet solitude.
Clear your mind of daily cares
And consciously release
All tensions, thoughts and worries
To create an inner peace.

When all is still and silent,
A restful, tranquil feeling
Facilitates reflection
And offers space for healing.
Let nature work its magic –
Breathe deeply, naturally;
And feel the power of silence:
Just sit and simply be.

– Emma Canning.

Friday — March 18

I HEARD of a hospital that places video screens above the patients' beds. The screens take their viewers on virtual walks along coastlines and through dappled forests. Earphones playing bird-song, sounds of the sea and the rustling of leaves complete the experience.

Apparently, the heightened sense of tranquillity eases pain and promotes recovery. I can very easily believe it.

So, let's wish the health boards and their patients all the best in what must be quite a costly venture. And as for the rest of us? Well, let's not forget that the original versions of the therapy – the woods, the coastline, the birds, the wildlife – are all out there for us to enjoy and benefit from. For free!

No video screens or headphones required.

Saturday — March 19

H AVE you ever not done something because you were afraid you might not do it right?

Robert Louis Stevenson told of a Father Damien who tried to help lepers on a South Sea island. He was completely incompetent – he had no idea how to run a hospital and was hopeless with money. Complaints were aired. Other agencies took over, nurses arrived. The lepers improved dramatically.

All of which, RLS insisted, was to the credit of Father Damien. People would never have come along to do better if he hadn't tried and failed first.

If you feel called to do something, but worry you can't, try anyway. Even if you fail, you might provide the world with a very necessary beginning.

Sunday — March 20

L IFE is all about give and take. This Sunday, these words are appropriate: God gives blessings to us in order that we can give glory to Him.

Monday — March 21

WISE heads tell us that our failures and trials can actually be blessings in disguise. But it's sometimes hard to believe.

Which was why I loved reading about Hollywood's first-ever official stunt-man. Frank Hanaway was known for his "skill" in falling off horses. What made it skilful was that he generally did it without hurting himself.

How did he develop that talent? Well, before getting into movies he was in the U.S. Cavalry – where I am guessing he fell off his horse a lot! No doubt the other soldiers laughed, but they probably envied him his career later.

So, next time you come down with a bump, don't despair. You might be developing a valuable skill!

Tuesday — March 22

LIEUTENANT COLONEL ALFRED WINTLE was a regular contributor to the letters page of "The Times". Then, in February 1946, he wrote saying, "Sir. I have just written you a long letter. On reading it over I have thrown it into the waste-paper basket. Hoping this meets with your approval."

A wise man or woman might have a lot to say on a wide variety of topics – but a wiser person knows when it's best to say nothing.

Wednesday — March 23

IF all my friends were to jump off a bridge, I wouldn't jump with them. I'd be at the bottom to catch them when they fall.'

"I can see what the writer means," the Lady of the House said when she saw that quote from an unknown author. "Even though we may not agree with the actions of our friends, we still have to allow them to make their own decisions. And if it all goes wrong, there's still something practical we can do to help."

I don't know who wrote that quotation, but I rather think that the writer – and the Lady of the House – have explained things perfectly!

Thursday — March 24

I **USED** to be indecisive, but now I'm not so sure."

It's an old quip, but still makes me smile, probably because, like so many of us presented with too much choice, I don't always find it easy to make up my mind.

But if those decisions happen to be important ones, then we can sometimes become so frightened of getting it wrong that we can't move forward at all.

Time, then, to take heart from the words of Spanish poet Antonio Machado who reminds us: "Traveller, there is no path. The path is made by walking."

If you feel lost in a maze of indecision, remember that your leap of faith is far more likely to get you there than someone else's map.

Friday — March 25

R **ANDOM** Acts of Kindness became an Internet craze in 2014. It began when one individual became disillusioned with all the pointless, nonsensical acts that people put online.

Residents in a small Scottish town were unexpectedly given flowers, cakes, sweets, even money. Older people were helped to cross busy roads, and were treated to other kind-hearted deeds by people they had never met before.

Why not perform an act of kindness to someone you don't know, today? You might make a good friendship as a result!

Saturday — March 26

T **HE** Lady of the House and I have just been guests at the wedding of a dear friend's daughter.

From the best man's speech, these words have remained in my mind: "Marriage is an empty box. It remains empty unless you put in more than you take out."

Wise counsel, I thought, for any married couple, young or old.

Sunday — March 27

WE thank you for this Easter, Lord,
As once more hope revives,
And for the beauty and the joy
You bring into our lives.
This season has a healing touch,
It eases heart and mind,
And we go forward hopefully,
The winter left behind.

We thank you for your promise, Lord,
We know that life goes on
And those we loved and thought were lost
Are never really gone.
They're all around us every day
To comfort and to guide
And when our path is steep and rough
They're always by our side.

So thank you, Lord, for love and light
To lead us on our way,
Please help us share
The hope and joy
And thank you for today.

– Iris Hesselden.

Monday — March 28

ON his seventieth birthday the poet Walt Whitman received a letter from the novelist Mark Twain. Twain congratulated him on all the wonders that had occurred during his lifetime and urged him to live a few more decades so he might see humanity reach its full potential; a time, he wrote, when it would be shown that "human wheat is worth more than human tares" (weeds).

That time has yet to come. Whitman didn't see it, and neither did Twain. But I should like to. Wouldn't you? Well . . . let's get busy weeding and see if we can't find a preview of that wonderful time in our own lives.

Beautiful Borders

48

Tuesday — March 29

A FRIEND of ours was telling us that the highlight of her week is a walk to her local convenience shop with her little grandson. Although it's only 200 yards away, it takes them about 20 minutes.

"That's because we stop every few yards," she said, "to examine the rosehips on the bushes and count the boulders lining the path (there are 14). Always one stone, indistinguishable to my eyes from the others, must be picked up and placed carefully in Granny's pocket." She laughed. "When his father was that age I was a busy mother, racing to the shops or to drop off at schools or playgroup. It's only now that I've been granted the gift of time."

As she went on her way I reflected how blessed grandparents are to share with these youngsters the wonders of the world . . . even if it's only on a short trip to the shops!

Wednesday — March 30

COUNTLESS societies and cults have come into being over the centuries based on secrets not, apparently, known to the general populace.

I'm guessing that if there really were such secrets they would most likely be "hidden" in plain sight, often overlooked because they are so obvious. The author Lewis Carroll must have been thinking along similar lines when he shared what he knew of such mysteries.

"One of the deep secrets of life," he wrote, "is that all that is really worth the doing is what we do for others!"

Thursday — March 31

I'M sure most of us know of Laura Ingalls Wilder as the author of the "Little House On The Prairie" books, stories of her life in pioneer America. But though her stories continue to delight, aren't they perhaps rather outdated now? Well, let us consider this quote from the author: "The real things haven't changed. It is still best to be honest and truthful; to make the most of what we have; to be happy with simple pleasures; and have courage when things go wrong."

No longer relevant? Well – you decide!

April

ROSIE was telling me about her nephew, who has just been appointed as a surgeon in a top hospital.

"He always did well at school," she told us, "which is why he found things hard when he first went to university."

I must have looked puzzled, for she explained.

"When you've never had to struggle to excel, it can be hard to discover that sometimes success doesn't just fall into your lap. Luckily, after his initial shock, Tim soon realised that perseverance brings its own rewards."

That story made me think of some words of Joe Girard, a famously successful American salesman, who wisely pointed out, "The elevator to success is out of order. You'll have to use the stairs . . . one step at a time."

Oh, well. It may take more puff, but we'll have certainly earned that view from the top!

OH, who cares what I think?"

We may think it's polite to keep our opinions to ourselves. And if those opinions are negative, then that's probably the best policy. But you never know who might take on a positive comment!

Eleven-year-old Gracie Bedell wrote to an aspiring politician telling him she liked him, but she was sure he would get more votes if only he grew a beard. Abraham Lincoln (who was, thereafter, hardly ever seen without a beard) sprouted some whiskers and won the election.

Did that letter make a difference? Well, it earned Gracie a visit from the President and a personal thank you!

So, if you have an opinion – positive ones only, please – get them out there. You might find that someone does care what you think!

Sunday — April 3

THEY say Queen Elizabeth the First once asked a merchant to undertake a long foreign mission for her. He balked at the prospect, protesting that his business would surely fail if he wasn't there to look after it.

Not an easy woman to say no to, Queen Elizabeth replied, "You, sir, take care of my business, and I will take care of yours."

When he returned years later he found that the association with the Queen had caused his business to grow beyond all expectation and he was now a very wealthy man.

Now, I'm not saying you should run away and neglect your work. But I am suggesting you put God's work first in your life – and see how everything else flourishes because of it.

Monday — April 4

THE Lady of the House and I live close to a devoutly Christian couple who have two young children. Every time we see them the parents are teaching the young ones right from wrong, reading to them and encouraging creative play.

The young mum once said to me during a conversation, "What you instil in your child's heart now creates their character for later."

A lovely, positive attitude, and one I heartily agree with.

Tuesday — April 5

DEAR friend, I never say aloud the words I'm writing here,
I never mention all the things that I should make more clear.
I take for granted you'll be there to pop round for a brew,
To help me find the perfect dress, or share a joke or two.
I never doubt, when I feel sad, you'll give support and cheer,
That should I feel the need to talk, you'll lend a listening ear.
I never speak these things aloud, but though I never say,
I value you, my steadfast friend, far more than words convey.
– Margaret Ingall.

Wednesday — April 6

HAVING been through a difficult time recently, Maureen's been very glad of the support of some wonderful friends.

"I just wish there was some way to repay them," she confided. "But at the moment, I just have to go by the words of Frank D. Sherman in his poem 'Friends': 'Since I have no gold to give, And love alone must make amends, My only prayer while I live, God make me worthy of my friends'."

An excellent sentiment! With such awareness, I have no doubt that Sherman, and indeed Maureen, are already entirely worthy. After all, true friendship has never been about material rewards, but those intangible qualities that are worth far more than money.

Thursday — April 7

FEELING a little imperfect? Not up to the job ahead? Big Ben (the bell behind the clock) has been ringing the hours and the quarter hours for over a century and a half. It's an audible symbol of London the whole world over.

And it has been cracked for almost all of that time!

Big Ben doesn't make the sound the foundry workers who cast it thought it ought to make. But it's a fine sound nonetheless!

Friday — April 8

HAVE you ever felt life is beyond your control? If so, be assured you aren't alone, for not one of us can truly claim to be in complete charge of our own circumstances.

It was pastor Charles Swindoll who remarked that "Life is ten per cent what happens to me, and ninety per cent how I react to it" – and I'm pretty sure that applies to the rest of humanity as well!

So let's make sure we concentrate on improving that 90 per cent, for our reactions are certainly something which we can do our best to control. And if we can manage to make those positive, well – there will be very little room left for the negative!

Saturday — April 9

"HOME, Sweet Home" and "Home is where the heart is". These two sayings have stood the test of time and speak volumes in a few words. Shakespeare wrote in "As You Like It": "When I was at home, I was in a better place."

May your home be your better place – always.

Sunday — April 10

THERE'S an old story of six young men applying for one job at the telegraph office. They all knew Morse code so they filled out the applications the secretary gave them with confidence. Then they all sat and waited to be called into the office for an interview.

A few minutes later one young man got up and walked into the office. The others were amazed at his nerve. But the secretary explained, "While you have all been sitting there, the telegraph was repeatedly tapping out a message. It said, 'If you can understand this, come in. You've got the job'."

The message was there for all of them. Each of them could have deciphered it. But only one was listening.

It's intriguing to think that the world, and everything in it, might be a message sent to each of us, inviting us to play a part in God's Grand Plan. Are you listening? Do you want the job?

Monday — April 11

AS I expect you know, I am a great believer in the philosophy that our biggest regrets in life usually arise from the chances we don't take, rather than the chances that we do. However, not all of us are as brave as we'd like to be, so for those who would prefer to start small, let's try this suggestion from the Indian spiritual teacher Osho.

"Whenever you have an opportunity to laugh, laugh; whenever you have an opportunity to dance, dance; whenever you have an opportunity to sing, sing – and one day you will find you have created your paradise."

Not so difficult or scary after all!

Tuesday — April 12

W HAT would you do if you could change the past?" our friend Mary asked. My mind was filled with possibilities. When I opened my mouth to speak she laughed and said, "It doesn't matter. Nobody can change the past. But we can change the future."

Of course I had to ask how we would set about doing such a thing.

"Easy," she explained. "Forgive someone. And both your futures will be changed for the better."

Wednesday — April 13

H ARD work and effort usually lead to success. But if success is what you are all about then you might be missing something.

There is no doubting that Bobby Pearce, the Australian rower, trained very hard in the run-up to the 1928 Olympic Games. In fact, in one of his races he was so far ahead of the others that when a family of ducks paddled in front of his one-man scull he had time to stop and let them pass, before going on to win the event.

Succeeding is fine, but sometimes the effort we put into it allows us a bonus – the chance to let a little grace into the race.

Thursday — April 14

A NEW day is born –
Wake up and give thanks,
New prospects, new dawn,
Make time to give thanks.
As sun gains in height,
Rejoice and give thanks
For each small delight.
It's time to give thanks.
As dusk starts to fall
Seek space to give thanks,
For God's love for all
With joy, offer thanks.

– Margaret Ingall.

Friday — April 15

WE came across this quotation recently and found it rather puzzling.

"To learn something new, take the path that you took yesterday."

Having considered this for a while, we began to understand a little better. How often have you travelled a route used many times and suddenly noticed something different? It could be a beautiful tree, a signpost at a road junction, or words of welcome outside a church.

As we grow older, we are ready to admit that we can still learn something new, every day. So don't be disappointed if you need to follow a regular route.

Keep looking and learning. There could be something quite new today! At times, what we can accomplish on our own seems little, but with a helping hand we can all achieve great things.

Saturday — April 16

IT'S so hard," Ellie complained, "to begin a job when you just can't see any end to it." Her words were, we felt, a slight exaggeration, for she was only grumbling about doing her school homework. Nevertheless, it did start us thinking about all those who really do embark upon a job which they know will never reach fruition in their lifetime.

"Like those who built the great cathedrals, knowing that they'd never see them finished," Ellie's mum said.

"Or the woodmen who plant forests," the Lady of the House put in.

"Or those who work for peace," I couldn't help adding. "They must know that mending the friction of centuries gone by can never happen overnight, yet still they keep trying."

At which point even Ellie had the grace to smile at her original complaints.

May God bless all those who have the faith to work on such long-term projects, for without them the world would indeed be a poorer place.

Sunday — April 17

IT was one of the most popular places in a festival set up to celebrate music and community. The giant blackboard had a sign above it saying, *Your Fears Erased Here Daily*. Each day the board would be covered by the scribbled worries of festival-goers and by each new morning they would be gone; washed off, every day, for a week.

Most of our fears are as transient as that. They exist largely in our imagination. But we tend to keep them around. Imagine if we could have a week when they were all wiped away for us!

Of course we could always turn to the Bible for longer lasting help. They do say it has a "do not fear" or "fear not" for every day of the year!

Monday — April 18

HE was right, you know," our friend Mary said, "but he wasn't!"

Not for the first time she had me at a loss. How could someone be right – but not right? So she explained an encounter she had witnessed when someone was entitled to say and do what he did, but the end result left nothing but unhappiness.

"When we make being right more important than being kind," Mary told me, "then we're wrong." She looked at me with that familiar twinkle in her eye. "Right?"

I, kindly, didn't argue.

Tuesday — April 19

WHAT'S the most valuable thing you possess, I wonder?

I don't imagine it's a question we actually ask ourselves often – unless we happen to be filling in an insurance claim form! But personally the query wouldn't call for much head-scratching on my part, for I think the best answer came from Goethe when he said, "Nothing is worth more than this day."

Yes, indeed – and what a privilege to have it at our disposal. I do hope that you enjoy owning yours!

Wednesday — April 20

*IT'S good to make plans for the future –
Ambition? A trait to admire.
At times we need targets to aim for,
And triumphs to which we aspire.*

*Yet often, contentment is realised
Not by dreams of what, when and how,
But simply by wishing for our lives
To be just the way they are now.*

— Emma Canning.

Thursday — April 21

IF there's one thing that is certain in life it is that, sooner or later, even the most upbeat and positive of us will find ourselves travelling through difficult times. James, who has had to cope with a long-term illness, told me his own mantra for helping him in times of need: nine simple words from Julian of Norwich: "God made me. God loves me. God keeps me."

May those same words bring light to your darkness, and hope to your journey.

Friday — April 22

I ADMIT it – I unashamedly enjoy searching out interesting quotes on the subject of friendship and, what's more, I equally enjoy sharing them with you! Here's my latest find and, although the author seems to be our good old friend Unknown, the words are well worth remembering:

"If you're alone, I'll be your shadow. If you want to cry, I'll be your shoulder. If you want a hug, I'll be your pillow. If you need to be happy, I'll be your smile. But any time you need a friend, I'll just be me."

And that's the best kind of friend of all.

Saturday — April 23

THE concept of paying it forward – taking a good deed done for you and passing it on to someone else – may seem like a modern phenomenon.

But it may actually have been invented in the 18th century by Benjamin Franklin.

Sending money to an acquaintance in need, he urged the man to give a similar amount to someone else whenever he was in a position to do so.

He hoped the future recipient would do the same, and so on, so it would pass "thro' many hands before it meets with a knave who will stop its progress.

"This is a trick of mine," Franklin continued, "for doing a deal of good with a little money. I am not rich enough to afford much in good works, and am obliged to be cunning and make the most of a little."

Would you like to do a deal of good? Then do a little – and send it on its way, Franklin style.

Sunday — April 24

AN important part of the Jewish Passover celebrations is the concept of Dayenu. It means something like, "that would have been enough."

They sing of the blessings God has bestowed on their people and, after each one, they sing "that would have been enough."

But, of course, there is always more to sing about.

I think if most of us were to take a moment to look back at our lives to when our blessings reached the point of being enough, we would find it lost in the mists of time – with every blessing since then being bonus upon bonus.

If we haven't said Dayenu yet then perhaps we ought to.

And we could follow that up with a thank you . . . for there always being more to sing about!

Monday — April 25

A FEW years back an American couple set out on pilgrimage to the home of Beatrix Potter. Used to long, straight highways they found the roads in the Lake District rather different. There seemed to be next to no signposts and the twists and turns in the road soon left them hopelessly confused. But they persevered and eventually found themselves at Hill Top.

Finding a National Trust employee, they complained about the lack of signs on the way. He turned and waved at the crowds of visitors and said, "Look how busy we are! Can you imagine what it would be like if we made it easier to get to?"

The point is that Hill Top *was* busy. Just like in life, if a thing is worth having – or getting to – people will find a way! And my American friends did.

Tuesday — April 26

WORDS of wisdom can come from many surprising places. So perhaps we shouldn't be surprised that the sea has some advice for us. It suggests that we –

> Be "shore" of ourselves,
> Take time to "coast",
> Avoid "pier" pressure,
> And "sea" life's beauty.

I wonder – was it really the sea who wrote those helpful words, or was it some anonymous beach-combing philosopher? Seems a bit "fishy" to me!

Wednesday — April 27

A FRIEND who had gone shopping in the city had witnessed a blazing argument between husband and wife, which had upset her immensely and she felt the need to confide in us about it.

"Surely," said the Lady of the House, "losing your temper is not a way to get rid of it."

Amen to that!

Thursday — April 28

*IT'S raining outside, and it's blowing a storm,
But here in my kitchen, it's cosy and warm.
I'm baking some biscuits, I'm rolling the dough,
I'm cutting the shapes and they're ready to go.
I glance at the window – just see how it rains!
The chill of the air is quite fogging the panes.
Now, back to the oven and yes, I can see
The biscuits are ready, so time now for tea.
With plate full of goodies, and mug in my hand,
Whatever the weather, my day's turned out grand!*

– Margaret Ingall.

Friday — April 29

SOMEONE once said, "There is always music among the trees."

On a windy day the trees give a whistling, sighing sound, with a mixture of notes. On a calm day the music among the trees is more likely to be the sound of birdsong and animal calls.

To hear it, head for the woods in the early morning or late evening when it's less likely that people will be there to disturb the music. And listen to the sounds of nature . . . and enjoy!

Saturday — April 30

WE try to stay in touch with the people who are important to us. When we meet them we try to give them a kind word; try to make them feel loved. Because we enjoy seeing the happiness on their faces, and because we mean it.

Life can be busy, though, and from time to time someone important gets neglected. I would go so far as to suggest someone you just couldn't do without is feeling a little neglected right now.

When was the last time you told yourself how much you appreciate you? You would love to hear it – and you would feel better for having said it. Especially when you see the smile you put on your face.

After all, you would do it for others!

May

ONCE more the rain is pouring down,
A grey and dismal day,
But see the trees, they're wonderful,
A magical display!
Once more the wind is blowing cold
And we all feel the chill,
But see the clouds go scurrying
Above that distant hill.

Once more the dark is creeping in
To chase away the light,
But see the stars, they're coming out
To watch us through the night.
Once more our plans have gone awry,
All we were hoping for,
But see a new tomorrow dawn,
Hold fast to dreams once more.

– Iris Hesselden.

THE great country singer Johnny Cash told of a childhood friend who had polio. On the three-mile walk from their homes to school some of the children would make fun of his hobbling walk.

"I imitated him, too, of course," Cash said, "but not that way. He's where I got my guitar style, playing rhythm and leading with my thumb." That style served him well in a music career spanning six decades.

Perhaps we shouldn't discourage our children from imitating other people but encourage them, like young John Cash, to copy only the best from each other.

Tuesday — May 3

GREAT philosophies aren't always found in books. Words of wisdom aren't always pronounced in speeches to vast crowds.

This particular piece of advice came skipping around the corner with our dear friend Mary. She came to a sudden halt in front of me, blushing and smiling.

She explained that some thoughtless soul had really annoyed her so she was taking her mother's advice.

"She told me that if ever I was angry I should try skipping – and I wouldn't be angry for long."

I wasn't angry but after we said our good-days I turned the corner and tried a curious little skip. All I can say is that Mary's mother should be up there with the wisest of women and the greatest of philosophers.

Wednesday — May 4

HAVE you ever put off doing something because it was too expensive, too far, too difficult, would take too long . . .?

Back when the Statue of Liberty was still in the design stage the builders ran out of money. So a publisher started a fund-raising drive. More than 120,000 people contributed – but most gave less than a dollar. You could say that mighty edifice was built a dollar at a time.

Never be daunted by the size of your dream. Focus on that first little step. Then the next. A dollar at a time, you'll get there!

Thursday — May 5

I WAS intrigued to discover someone had written "A Natural History Of Enthusiasm." Isaac Taylor's 1829 volume wasn't what I expected. It was a fictional history of the church and its various leaps forward. Interesting, but imagine if someone was to write a modern treatise on enthusiasm. A life well lived surely offers many subjects to be enthusiastic about.

In which categories would your passions earn you a footnote? Or on which subjects would you be cited as an enthusiastic expert?

Carpet Of Bluebells

Friday — May 6

WHEN Hilary retired from her bustling office, although she loved her new-found freedom, it wasn't very long before she realised how much she missed her colleagues and the camaraderie of having a sense of purpose.

"But luckily," she told me, "a friend of mine was involved in a local charity, and before I knew what I was doing, I'd been roped in to help." She laughed. "It was just like the words of teacher and artist Mbali Creazzo: 'Giving of any kind, taking an action, begins the process of change, and moves us to remember that we are part of a much greater universe'."

And it's hard to feel lonely when you're part of a whole universe!

Saturday — May 7

THE painter Henri Matisse once said, "There is nothing more difficult for an artist to paint than a rose. First he has to forget every other rose he has ever seen."

You have to take a similar approach when getting to know people, I think. Now, I'm not suggesting you forget every other person you have ever met. I'm suggesting you remember that each one of them – regardless of how many people you have met – will be special in their own unique way.

Sunday — May 8

I CAME across this short prayer, written anonymously:
Before you sleep, gently lay
All your fears and angst away;
Place your worries and your care
In the trusting hands of prayer.

Say this prayer tonight and sleep peacefully, knowing that God never sleeps.

Monday — May 9

T was the sight of a poster promoting an investment scheme that prompted Anne's remark.

"The habit of saving," she pronounced sagely, "is sometimes overrated."

Seeing my bemusement, she smiled.

"Coming from a poor family," she explained, "I was brought up to be aware that I should always keep something in reserve for the future. And so I did – until one day a friend gave me some chocolate for my birthday.

"I duly put it safely aside – only to find that it had gone mouldy before I could enjoy it! Nowadays I've come to realise that however sensible it is to save, sometimes the good things in life need to be enjoyed right here and now."

Wise words, I think. I firmly believe that there are times when we really do have to seize the moment, and just to prove the point, I'm off to enjoy the sunshine – something which fortunately can never be put aside to go mouldy!

Tuesday — May 10

WHEN the bills are hitting the doormat
And the sky is black with rain,
We should pause and remember the things that we love
Until life feels better again.

A little child, wide-eyed with wonder,
A new puppy licking our chin,
A mistle thrush singing his song to the wind,
The smell of the earth after rain.

The perfume of roses at twilight,
Or walking barefoot in the sand,
The reflections of moonlight on water,
The touch of a loving friend's hand.

– Eliza Barret.

Wednesday — May 11

MY neighbour, Margaret, was telling me that she had become a volunteer gardener in our local public park. Margaret's garden puts the rest of the street to shame, so I knew they'd be glad to have her. But Margaret said the best bit was when the local primary school children come to visit and she gets to help them with their projects.

Helping those children gives Margaret even more pleasure than the gardening! And isn't that the same for most of us? Looking at the world anew through their fresh eyes can make the sun come out on a very cloudy day!

Thursday — May 12

I HAVE to be honest – it's not at all often that the Lady of the House passes on beauty tips to me! However, I was more than happy to be the recipient of her latest gleanings, as encapsulated in some advice attributed to Audrey Hepburn.

"For beautiful eyes, look for the good in others; for beautiful lips, speak only words of kindness; and for poise, walk with the knowledge that you are never alone."

Hmm. Don't tell, but I shall definitely try that out!

Friday — May 13

IT was thought that the Innocent Railway near Edinburgh was so named because no-one had ever been hurt on it.

The man who coined the name, Dr Robert Chalmers, suggested it was more to do with operating under horse-power when everyone else was using steam and that the journeys, which were full of "incident and adventure," never held "the least jeopardy".

Passengers, he wrote, had the chance to examine crops by the rail-side, hear the news from their fellow travellers and enjoy the banter of the officials which "never failed to delight".

If we can compare a railway trip to living, then I would happily travel that kind of "innocent" life.

Saturday — May 14

OUR friend Mary has occasional aches in her shoulders, elbows and fingers. Well, she's not the youngest person I know and I am all too aware that old age doesn't come by itself. But, even so, I should have known better than to suggest it was arthritis.

"It's an R.S.I.," she insisted. "A repetitive strain injury."

I was confused.

"What could you possibly do so often that would cause a strain in all those different joints?" I asked.

By way of an answer she reached out and hugged me.

Having completely proven her point, she smiled sweetly and went about her day.

Sunday — May 15

THE author E.B. White once received a letter from a fan who deplored the general condition of society. White responded that he was personally battling against the forces of chaos. How? By faithfully winding up his seven-day clock every Sunday!

It may sound like a flippant remark but, really, it is faith and diligence in the little things that make the big difference. So let's all join in the battle for a better tomorrow, improving the world one tick, or tock, at a time.

Monday — May 16

NOW – attention, please. Will all those of you who live an entirely simple and uncomplicated life kindly raise your hand? Ah – just as I thought. Not a single hand in the air, and that includes my own. Which means that almost inevitably we occasionally find ourselves so busy concentrating on the immediate difficulties that we lose sight of where we really want to be.

If you happen to be in that situation right now, think of the words of Ralph Waldo Emerson: "Don't be pushed by your problems. Be led by your dreams."

Tuesday — May 17

THE Lady of the House tried to reassure a friend who was finding things rather difficult.

There were certain aspects of this person's life that she desperately needed to give up in order to move forward, but she looked on the situation as a defeat.

We passed on these words to her and hoped they would be a comfort.

"Giving up doesn't always mean that you are weak. Sometimes it means that you are strong enough to let go."

I think these are words which we should all bear in mind when battling with life's problems.

Wednesday — May 18

NOW, here's a question for you – are you alive?

I'm smiling as I write this, imagining all my kindly readers scratching their heads.

"What on earth is Francis on about? Of course I'm alive!"

Yes, I was joking, of course – but the reason I ask is because I've just happened across some very profound words of African-American Howard Thurman.

He said, "Don't ask what the world needs. Ask what makes you come alive, and go do it. Because what the world needs is people who have come alive."

This really made me think about the people I know that this sentiment applies to. And it made me wonder if I couldn't be doing more about joining their number!

Howard Thurman was a writer, philosopher and theologian who used his many talents to establish the first racially integrated church in America, and worked hard for the Civil Rights Movement.

"Are you alive?"

Somehow I don't think that that is a question I would have had to ask him.

Thursday — May 19

HAVE you noticed," Frank observed, "how sometimes we humans are only too glad to find that we are 'too late' to do things? Too late to join that team of volunteers, too late to get involved with a protest group, too late to offer help – in fact 'too late' to do anything that might cost us a little time or trouble."

He grinned rather ruefully.

"Francis, I think that in future I shall ban those two words from my vocabulary, and try to do what I can as soon as I know I'm needed."

Frank's words reminded me of a proverb I once heard, which says: "The best time to plant a tree is twenty-five years ago. The second-best time is today."

Which goes some way to prove that, actually, it's never too late.

Friday — May 20

IN a world that seems to be increasingly appearance-orientated we could do worse than teach our little ones this philosophy by children's writer Roald Dahl:

"You can have a wonky nose and a crooked mouth and a double chin and stick-out teeth, but if you have good thoughts they will shine out of your face like sunbeams and you will always look lovely."

And if any of us older ones recognise a physical trait or two there, well, now we know what to do about them!

Saturday — May 21

GROWING up, I was often enthralled by my grandfather's tales of his times as a young man, when he was in the RAF, or when he played in the rugged world of amateur football.

But he knew the importance of memories, and as he was telling me his stories he was sharing a piece of his past, his heart, with me, which made the present we had together all the richer.

As for the future, whether you are with family, friends or by yourself, there are always more memories to draw from, creating something special each and every day.

Sunday — May 22

SOMETIMES when we're lonely and we long to hear God's voice,
Or troubled and uncertain and afraid to make a choice,
And no-one seems to listen, and the heavens all stay dumb,
Then how can we keep trusting, when no answers seem to come?

Fear not, for still He hears us; we can never slip His gaze,
He loves and reassures us in a thousand different ways,
He speaks with many voices – if we're patient and aware
We'll surely hear His answers, and we'll know we're in His care.
– Margaret Ingall.

Monday — May 23

THERE'S a story of a boy selling apples on a train. He walked from
the front to the back of the train, calling out in each carriage,
"Who will buy a juicy apple?"

No-one did.

But a finely dressed wealthy man in the last carriage took an apple,
polished it up, and walked the length of the train eating it. The boy,
following behind him, sold all his apples.

May those of us who need it find someone to lead the way.
And may those of us who are in a position to add a little shine to
someone else's efforts do so.

Tuesday — May 24

A GARDEN in full bloom might look like it sprang effortlessly into
glory – but it almost certainly didn't. There will generally have
been months of cultivation the passing admirer knows nothing about.

It's a rather similar story with those people who seem to have the
effortless knack of making people happy. Those good souls will tell
you there is nothing effortless about what they do.

The novelist Marcel Proust referred to their "spadework" when he
wrote, "Let us be grateful to the people who make us happy; they
are the charming gardeners who make our souls blossom."

Wednesday — May 25

WHAT would you give to see a miracle (apart from the ordinary, everyday ones that surround us continuously)?

Would you pay for it in discomfort? Because whether it's running out of wine at a wedding or parting a sea to escape a pursuing army, God only sends the showier kind of miracles at times of need.

Corrie ten Boom summed this up when she wrote, "He uses our problems for His miracles. That was my first lesson in learning to trust Him completely."

So, look for something special in your times of need. Trust – and stand by!

Thursday — May 26

I **TOOK** *the road less travelled*
To see what I might find,
To search for hope and seek for joy
And quiet peace of mind.
The long, smooth road that beckoned me,
It seemed to be the one,
It led to far horizons
Where many thoughts had gone.
It went through woods and open fields
Where I could be alone,
To plan my plans and dream my dreams
And call the world my own.
It left behind all past mistakes
When many things went wrong,
It led me on to sunlit skies
And in my heart a song.
So take the road that beckons you
Enjoying every mile,
Discover hope and happiness.
The journey is worthwhile!

– Iris Hesselden.

Friday — May 27

"DO you miss it, Francis?" the Lady of the House asked.

We had paused to watch a young couple, very much in love, walk by. He was handsome, she was beautiful. And they were young.

I protested that I wasn't old enough to miss youth yet and she laughed. Then, by way of reassurance, she quoted the Polish poet Stanislaw Lec.

"Youth is a gift of nature but age is a work of art."

I assured her I would get painting – one of these days. But Mr Lec had it right – what we are in younger years we have little control over, but what we are in later years often depends on what we make of ourselves. Let's make something beautiful.

Saturday — May 28

"SMILES," the cynic might say, "they are fleeting, cost nothing, what good can they possibly do?"

At first glance Joseph Addison, the 18th-century poet and playwright, might agree.

"These are trifles, to be sure," he said, referring to those happy expressions, "but scattered along life's pathway the good they do is inconceivable."

Sunday — May 29

THERE'S a ledge on a rock-face in Yosemite National Park called the Thank God Ledge.

Some say it's so named because the forty-foot-long ledge is the only way across the mountain. Others suggest that if you have the courage to stand up on the two-foot-wide ledge you can see God's beautiful creation laid out in front of you and you can't help but thank Him. A third opinion is that everyone who makes it across the ledge without falling 1800 feet automatically thanks God!

Me? I can thank God for a clear route ahead, the wonders of creation, and a safe journey right here at sea-level, thank you very much!

Monday — May 30

DURHAM Cathedral has an ancient tradition of sanctuary. In times gone by a monk would sit in a window above the door, looking out.

Anyone being pursued by enemies, or creditors, and who grabbed hold of the iron ring of the door knocker, would be granted four weeks to sort things out, or to leave the country peacefully.

In a world where we can sometimes feel under all sorts of pressures the idea of sanctuary might seem a very attractive one. But the tradition has no legal standing any more.

So, should the whole concept of sanctuary simply be relegated to history?

I would suggest not; not while each of us might take the place of the monk in the window, looking out for someone in need of respite, a helping hand, and a little time out from their troubles.

Tuesday — May 31

HMM," Lenny said, as he surveyed his vegetable patch. "Those carrots are very late coming up, and I'm not sure the beans are looking as good as they might."

I had to hide a smile, for Lenny is notoriously unduly pessimistic about his burgeoning crops. I have known him a long time and I have never heard him sound upbeat about his predicted harvest.

What he doesn't dwell upon is the fact that he's a regular green-fingered volunteer, helping any elderly and infirm neighbours with digging and watering, and sharing his crops with them.

He's also well known for passing on his knowledge and skill to children at the junior school – inspiring many of them to continue gardening long after they have left its doors.

In fact, thinking about Lenny, I could almost imagine this quotation from Robert Louis Stevenson was written especially for him:

"Don't judge each day by the harvest you reap, but by the seeds that you plant."

And there's nothing to be pessimistic about there, Lenny!

June

HAVE you heard of "The Children's Encyclopaedia"? The first instalment appeared in 1908, priced 7d. The story goes that Arthur Mee's little daughter Marjorie was always asking questions. Her harassed mother once exclaimed, "Oh, for a book that answers all these questions!"

And the Encyclopaedia was born.

Marjorie, like most youngsters, was described as a "child of wonder", an epithet later applied to her father.

"The Children's Encyclopedia" was published monthly for 25 years and probably still didn't answer all the questions children ask.

It's that kind of world. No matter how much we know there is always more to be fascinated by. So, let's walk through this life as Mr Mee and Marjorie did, constantly appreciating, constantly marvelling, fully entitled to call ourselves children of wonder.

JANE felt like a square peg in a round hole.

"I didn't much like my job, and wasn't even very good at it," she confessed. "But I was afraid to leave. Then one day," she continued, "I happened to pick up a magazine which contained an article about a sheepdog. Despite its pedigree, the dog turned out to be hopeless at herding sheep. It was only later that the farmer realised, when it came to rounding up the hens and ducks each evening, the dog was perfect at the job!"

Jane laughed.

"It may sound silly, but that article prompted me to act. Now I've changed jobs, I feel I'm really using my gifts."

Good for Jane – and a timely reminder that we all have our own talents – even if they do turn out to be rather unexpected!

Friday — June 3

WE tend, more and more these days, to think there is a solution to every problem. In more difficult times a more pragmatic approach was needed and an unknown poet penned advice that might yet be of use to us.

"For every ill beneath the sun
There is some remedy – or none;
If there be one, resolve to find it;
If not, submit, and never mind it!"

Saturday — June 4

YOU want to find friends,
But they seem all too rare?
Whenever you need one,
There's nobody there?
Perhaps you are starting
The wrong way around,
For I know a way
They'll be easily found –
Just first be a friend;
Show you're caring and kind,
And suddenly – look –
They're so easy to find!

– Margaret Ingall.

Sunday — June 5

THE English Puritan minister Richard Baxter, who lived in the 17th century, was a serious theologian. You can tell that from the titles of some of his 141 books, like "A Call To The Unconverted To Turn That They Might Live", "The Saints' Everlasting Rest" and – "The Life Of Mrs Margaret Baxter"! If that last one seems out of place, then think again. He wrote it so the world would know of his wife, her virtues, and her tendernesses. And I am sure there was as much, if not more, of God's love in their marriage than might be found in any weighty theological tome.

Golden Glory

Monday — June 6

"SOMETIMES," Lesley said, "when I read the newpapers or watch television, I get quite depressed by just how cynical some people seem to be. That's why I was really encouraged to find this quote from Harvey Fierstein, the American actor and playwright. He said, 'I do believe we're all connected. I do believe in positive energy. I do believe in the power of prayer. I do believe in putting good out into the world. And I believe in taking care of each other.' "

A well-found quote indeed, Lesley – for if more of us believe in those things, then I believe that there is not much wrong with the world!

Tuesday — June 7

"IF you want to get ahead," Tommy told me, "you should be like a kangaroo."

Like most ten-year-olds, Tommy goes to school, but his passion for books leads to a lot of extra-curricular learning. Of course, I asked what he meant.

"Well, those powerful back legs and tail make it nearly impossible for a kangaroo to go backwards. Whatever direction they travel in they always have to be moving forward."

"A very good point," I conceded. "Now you should move forward to school before the bell rings. And dare I suggest that you hop to it?"

Wednesday — June 8

ARE you having a bit of a boring day today? Well, I suppose it can happen to the best of us from time to time – but when it does, I strongly suggest you take a piece of advice from William Arthur Ward.

He said, "Lose yourself in generous service and every day can be a most unusual day, a triumphant day, an abundantly rewarding day!"

Now, that does sound like a day worth having!

Thursday — June 9

THE "glamorous" life of a Hollywood actress involved a lot of time on-set but off-camera. Elizabeth Taylor recalled one game she used to play with the writers and fellow actors. The question was, "If there was to be a sign hung above your life that would perfectly describe it, what would it say?" You didn't get to choose your own sign. Those who knew you chose for you.

Some of the answers were risqué, some were insightful, others were funny. But, away from the bright lights and the make-up, it's a question each of us might ask.

What would the sign for your life say? And would you be a "diva" or a "legend"?

Friday — June 10

OUR old friend Mary lives in a charming country cottage with a beautifully tended and cleverly planted garden which is her pride and joy. When the Lady of the House complimented Mary on her dazzling display of flowers, Mary commented: "My garden helps me to restore all my senses. I'd be much worse off without it."

I think that would apply to many of us.

Saturday — June 11

THE Historical Group were portraying the Land Girls of WWII. Six ladies in dungarees and headscarves sang a song from the period. The first verse was about milking the cows, the next was about feeding the pigs, followed by a verse about driving a tractor.

The last line of each verse was, "My word, we are winning the war!" And they were – just not in the most obvious way!

The song was played for laughs, but the important message behind it is that big battles can be won by taking care of the little details.

So, if you have a difficult obstacle to overcome, increase your chances of winning by making sure you have, metaphorically, fed the ducks, rubbed down the horses, and gathered in the eggs!

Sunday — June 12

I WAS lucky," Laura said. "In our family we always had Great-aunt Dorothy to turn to."

She'd been telling us about this remarkable lady. Orphaned in her teens, she had spent her youth bringing up her younger siblings, becoming their anchor. And she'd continued in that role as they grew into adults, married and produced their own families.

"Outsiders might not have realised it," Laura said, "but to us she was the heart of the family, steady, wise, and very much loved."

What a wonderful tribute. Her life reminds me of some thoughts of David Grayson: "Contentment, and indeed usefulness, come as the infallible result of great acceptances, great humilities – of not trying to make ourselves this or that, but of surrendering ourselves to the fullness of life – of letting life flow through us."

May all Great-aunt Dorothys come to know just how much they are cherished!

Monday — June 13

STELLA had been chatting to me about what first led her into undertaking voluntary work with several local charities.

"Well," she admitted, "I used to get so depressed at all the bad news in the papers that I made conscious efforts not to care. Thankfully, I eventually realised that even if I couldn't change the world, at least I could make a difference nearer home. Nowadays, I get involved and try to make things better."

Stella's experience brought to mind some thought-provoking words of Elie Wiesel, who was both a Holocaust survivor and Nobel Peace Prize winner.

He said, "The opposite of love is not hate, it's indifference. The opposite of art is not ugliness, it's indifference. The opposite of faith is not heresy, it's indifference. And the opposite of life is not death, it's indifference."

But the wonderful thing is that indifference can be overcome.

Let's start now!

Tuesday — June 14

I HEARD of a school inspector who looked over a little lad's shoulder and saw the following written on his jotter –

Yesterday, yesterday, yesterday
Sorrow, sorrow, sorrow
Tomorrow, tomorrow, tomorrow
Love, love, love.

"What a beautiful poem!" the inspector exclaimed.

"Dinna be daft," the lad replied. "It's my spelling list!"

Ah . . . but beauty and poetry will often be found in some very surprising places!

Wednesday — June 15

WHAT are the ingredients that make up a man? And how are they best shown, in his words or his actions?

Talking about the great actor Paul Newman, the playwright Tennessee Williams said,

"You never really know what he's thinking or what he might do – but it always ends in kindness and fairness. A mighty recipe produced this man."

Whatever ingredients make up our individual "recipes" we should try to make sure our actions are just as "tasty".

Thursday — June 16

"LIFE is what you make it," the old maxim goes. And there is a lot of truth in it.

But oftentimes there are situations beyond our control, which is when I prefer the words of the Emperor and philosopher Marcus Aurelius. "Life," he said, "is what our thoughts make it."

And so we can make a humble house seem a palace and a poor meal seem a feast – if we think it so!

Friday — June 17

JOHN CHAPMAN – also known as Johnny Appleseed – achieved near legendary fame by planting apple orchards across the still-expanding United States. He believed apples, with their promise of countless edible harvests, were a symbol of hope.

He also carried books with him on his travels, usually of the uplifting and inspirational type. If he found anyone in need of cheer he would cut out pages, even chapters, and make a gift of them.

Fruit and books were Johnny Appleseed's way of planting seeds of encouragement. With a little imagination we could surely do the same.

Saturday — June 18

ELVIS had the hit with it. Carl Perkins wrote it. Johnny Cash suggested it. But it was C.V. White, an American airman with no shoes but his uniform ones to go dancing in, who imagined those regulation black leather shoes were something a little more stylish. Then he told Cash (also in the Air Force at the time) not to step on his blue suede shoes.

Like C.V. White, we can aspire to better when we're in unsatisfactory situations. Have your dreams, take them dancing, even – and don't let anyone step on them.

Sunday — June 19

I LIKE being alone. Don't you? If you disagree, then please don't think us anti-social. I understand what D.H. Lawrence meant when he talked of the "sheer delight of being alone": how it helped him better appreciate things like the moon, an ash-tree, or the breeze.

But then he wrote a poem about it so he could share those experiences with the world. His unsociability became very social, and I understand that, too.

Let us not always be in solitude – and not always in company. Enjoy both for their unique blessings and you will find that each enhances the other!

C HOICE. It's a funny sort of thing.

Sometimes, when buying goods or choosing holidays, we seem to have more than enough of it – an abundance, in fact! Unfortunately, in other circumstances, we find to our cost that this isn't always the case.

There are times in most of our lives when events conspire to limit us – but at least we all have choice over our thoughts.

It was Dutch minister Henri J. M. Nouwen who said, "We can be unhappy about many things, but joy can still be there.

"It is important to become aware that at every moment of our life we have an opportunity to choose joy . . . It is in the choice that our true freedom lies, and that freedom is, in the final analysis, the freedom to love."

I suppose it's true to say that we choose our own attitude, and it's good to know that whatever our circumstances, we need never be separated from the most important things of all.

Tuesday — June 21

W HEN Dan and Hannah took their small son Jacob with them for a country walk, they were unaware of quite how steep the path up the wooded hillside would turn out to be.

Jacob kept going manfully until finally pausing to ask, "Daddy, does this road go right up to Heaven?"

We laughed at the story, but afterwards I couldn't help thinking that there was definite food for thought in those words.

Sometimes our own path through life does indeed seem too steep to be managed, and we often feel far too unprepared to tackle it – but oh, the rewards that await us if we can just manage to keep going.

And just in case you are wondering, yes – with a valiant effort and a fair bit of encouragement, little Jacob did manage to make it to the top!

May all of us be just as trustful and persevering.

Wednesday — June 22

MOTHER TERESA of Calcutta had her own understanding of joy. She described it as prayer, love, a net of love by which you can catch souls. A joyful heart, she said, is the inevitable result of a heart aflame with love.

May you have joy within you, today and every day.

Thursday — June 23

IN the garden of the heart
Grow seeds of love and trust;
Where honesty proliferates,
Where all is kind and just.
A garden warm and comforting,
Welcoming and splendid,
Where those who gladly step inside
Are nurtured and defended.

A garden that will fortify:
Compassionate and sweet,
A place of strength and tenderness –
A sure and safe retreat.
In the garden of the heart –
Enwrapped in love and grace –
Is where those who are dear to us
Will always hold a place.

– Emma Canning.

Friday — June 24

ON being asked about her legacy, the dancer Martha Graham said it was made up of little pieces, a day at a time. Her advice to get through each new day might, I think, apply equally to any of us.

"Get through the next twenty-four hours," she said, "as brilliantly, as truthfully, as clearly, and as kindly as you possibly can."

And my little addition to that? Let's make a dance of our dance – whether we can dance or not!

ELIZABETH HARRISON taught teachers professional standards in the late 19th century. She started off teaching young children so she knew what she was talking about.

A Nobel Peace Prize winner once said of her that she "did more good than any woman I know. She brought light and power to all the educational world."

How did she do all that? Well, through decades of hard work and perseverance. But, the personal philosophy at the core of her work might serve any one of us who would make a difference for the better.

It was simply this – "Those who are lifting the world upward and onward are those who encourage more than they criticise."

Sunday — June 26

WHEN I became a man I put away childish things," the Good Book says. Of course, some of us hold on to souvenirs of good times but we can often be too attached to things. A life well lived will have many stages and if we insist on holding on to material goods from each stage we will soon become weighed down by them.

The people we meet, on the other hand, are a different prospect and shouldn't be easily put away. Hollywood icon Audrey Hepburn summed the difference up beautifully when she said, "The best thing to hold on to in this life is each other."

Monday — June 27

LET us consider this message in verse from William Blake:
"It is right it should be so, Man was made for joy and woe.
And when this we rightly know, Thro' the world we safely go."

What Blake was trying to tell us was that in order to experience happiness in our life, we must also endure some pain.

But may today be a happy one for you.

Tuesday — June 28

COME away to the quiet fields,
Where the air is fresh, the sky is vast
And leave the world and all its woes
And all the problems of the past.
Come away as the stars appear
And there discover peace of mind,
Then, in the silence, rest awhile
And leave all troubled thoughts behind.
Come away and leave all care
And let your tranquil thoughts roam free,
Renew your strength, your hopes and dreams
Oh, come now, come away with me!

– Iris Hesselden.

Wednesday — June 29

PEG BRACKEN, who wrote humorous lifestyle books for women, once said, "If you write to someone twice a week there is so much to tell: twice a year and there is hardly a thing."

I would take that letter-writing tip and offer it as advice on how to live a life. Pay attention once in a while and it will seem like nothing much ever happens; live in the moment and you will never be short of interesting things to write to your friends about.

Thursday — June 30

THREE walkers met in a park. A bird began singing in a nearby tree and the first man named its species. But the second man insisted that species didn't live in the area. A bit of a debate ensued. The first man said he had a bird book in his car that would settle the matter. So they made for the car park.

The third man walked towards the tree and lost himself for a moment or two in the beauty of the unknown bird's song.

Which was the wisest: the man who knew, the man who knew better, or the man who took the moment for what it was and enjoyed it – whatever it was?

July

I COULDN'T help wondering why Alison was photographing her garden. Don't get me wrong, it was a pretty array of colours, but was she entering it into a competition or something like that?

"I enjoy my garden in the summer-time," she explained. "But I take the photos for the winter-time. I have them made into cards and then, when the weather has been particularly bleak, I send them to people I think might enjoy a little bit of summer."

J.M. Barrie's line, "God gave us our memories so we might have roses in winter," immediately came to mind. But it seems that a camera and the good heart of a good friend can help with that, as well.

Saturday — July 2

I KNOW I've never met you,
Yet still it seems to me
We've been good friends for ever,
As close as we can be.
We're bound by words on paper
Held fast through many years,
Since first we wrote as children,
Exchanging hopes and fears.
From teens till grown to adults,
From beaux to wedding rings,
From making homes and babies,
We've talked of many things.
And now, as we grow older,
Our letters bind us still,
For distance is as nothing
When bridged by true goodwill.

– Margaret Ingall.

Sunday — July 3

"IF I forgive them am I just letting them away with it?"

It's the unspoken doubt that often causes our better instincts to hesitate. The answer is – of course you are, but you're setting a powerful example in the process; an example that might do them the world of good.

I'm reminded of that lesson by these lines from the great poet Alfred, Lord Tennyson –

"For all the blessed souls in Heaven

Are both forgivers and forgiven."

Monday — July 4

TELLING the tale of Nicholas Nickleby in 1839, Charles Dickens wrote, "They kept on, with unabated perseverance, and the hill has not yet lifted its face to heaven that perseverance will not gain the summit of at last."

It took another 114 years before Tenzing Norgay and Edmund Hillary stood on the summit of Mount Everest but, writing like that, Dickens must always have believed that someone would!

No-one ever said perseverance was a fast option – but it's what will get you there in the end.

Tuesday — July 5

I LOVE it when conversations of no importance suddenly become something more.

Mary and I were chatting about this, that and nothing at all when our attentions were caught by a bird in song. It was clear, captivating and obviously nearby. We peered into the nearby trees hoping to see the winged deliverer of such delightful music. But the foliage was too thick.

"It doesn't matter," Mary said. "If life has taught me one thing it's that I don't have to see the source of my blessings to appreciate and enjoy them."

Feathered Friend

Wednesday — July 6

"WHAT a wonderful life I've had! I only wish I'd realised it sooner."
Those words came from the French novelist Colette, and I'm sure they were spoken with a smile. I'm glad she felt such pleasure in looking back on her existence, but I do think there's food for thought in that second sentence. So often we dwell on our current trials and challenges, rather than recognising and appreciating all the good things that happen, too. If we can manage to do that at the time, as well as being pleased about them in retrospect, well then – we shall have enjoyed our life twice over! Hurrah!

Thursday — July 7

DO you have hopes and dreams in your heart? Some special, secret thoughts that warm your soul? Perhaps you tell yourself on dull and disappointing days that they will never come true.

Hold fast to them as Louisa May Alcott did when she wrote these words: "Far away there in the sunshine are my highest aspirations. I may not reach them, but I can look up and see their beauty, believe in them, and follow where they lead."

Keep looking up and believing, and see their beauty. Who knows where they will lead?

Friday — July 8

DO you have letters after your name? O.B.E.? M.B.E.? D.B.E.? I am reminded of a children's magazine which, during WWI, encouraged the little ones to add the letters O.P.K after their names.

In dark evenings the street lamps often went unlit. After a rainy day, litter left underfoot could be a hazard, especially slippery things like orange peel. Children, out and about during the day, were encouraged to kick peel (and other potential hazards) into the gutter and so become Orange Peel Kickers. In their own way the OPKs were making the world as they found it a little better.

Surely a philosophy worthy of being included on the official honours list.

Saturday — July 9

I'VE never known a friendly word that's ever gone astray,
For friendly words are funny things – they hang around all day.
They creep inside the saddest heart, they lift a frame of mind,
They change harsh thoughts or feelings into actions far more kind.
They slide inside awareness; they bring balm to heal the soul,
They strengthen us and nourish, and they help to make us whole.
So never fight the impulse just to pause and say, "Hello!"
For friendly words work magic – far more magic than we know.
                                           – Margaret Ingall.

Sunday — July 10

"AMAZING GRACE" is a most uplifting hymn and aptly named, too, for God's grace is indeed amazing. But it's also mysterious. How do we begin to describe grace – other than that almost indefinable knowledge that we are loved, accepted, and forgiven our mistakes?

Thus I very much like the thoughts of Anne Lamott who admits, "I do not at all understand the mystery of grace – only that it meets us where we are, but does not leave us where it found us."

Perhaps that's the secret. "Grace will lead me home" say the words of the hymn. It only needs us to walk forward in trust.

Monday — July 11

I WONDER if you know the song "Whistle While You Work"? I will be surprised if you don't, for its lively tune and upbeat message have ensured its popularity over a good many years now. I always smile when I listen to it, despite once overhearing someone grumpily remark that it hardly matters whether one tackles a task in a happy or miserable frame of mind, "for the work still has to be done."

No, I'm much more in agreement with Thomas Carlyle, who wrote: "Wondrous is the strength of cheerfulness, and its power of endurance. The cheerful man will do more in the same time, will do it better and will preserve it longer, than the sad or sullen."

So there!

Tuesday — July 12

SHARON was in thoughtful mood.

"Isn't it funny how people can be so different," she mused. "Last year two new members of staff came to work in our office. Jill was bouncy and enthusiastic, and I knew we'd have lots in common. Hilary was much more reserved, and I wasn't at all sure how things would work out.

"But now – well, I still get on very well with Jill, but it's Hilary who has turned out to be the person I would call on whenever I was in need."

I think it was Socrates who said, "Be slow to fall into friendship but, when you are in, continue firm and constant." And in the intervening two and a half thousand years, I don't think anyone's put it better!

Wednesday — July 13

I OVERHEARD a couple contemplating life and holidays. As philosophers go, I rather think he was on the theoretical side and she was more on the practical. Which of them was the wiser I wouldn't like to say.

Man – "Instead of spending all our lives focused on our next holiday we should focus on creating the sort of life we don't want to take a break from."

Wife – "That sounds like a lot of work."

Man – "Mmm."

Wife – "We would probably need a holiday after all that."

Thursday — July 14

AT the end of this day, may I suggest that you write down all the good things you have in your life. This will very probably help you to have a good night's sleep and subconsciously set you up for a good day tomorrow. We should all count our blessings, and think positively.

In Dublin's Fair City

Friday — July 15

THE great jazz singer and trumpet player Louis Armstrong explained that one of the most important ingredients in his music was, "The memory of things gone. Things like old folks singing in the moonlight in the back yard on a hot night, or something said long ago."

Bearing in mind that we never know who might be listening, or what budding musician might be watching, wouldn't it be wonderful to live our lives in such a way that moments taken from it might inspire the music of the generation to come?

Saturday — July 16

I WONDER how many books, DVDs and courses there are running at any one time, teaching people how to live happier lives or achieve personal fulfilment. More than I could count, probably. And very few of them will be free.

The fact that so many people will pay so much money for them shows how important those attributes are. But, like most of the important things in life, there is a way of achieving them – for free!

Epictetus, the Greek slave turned philosopher, gave the secret away nearly 2,000 years ago. "Happiness and personal fulfilment," he wrote, "are the natural consequences of doing the right thing."

Sunday — July 17

IN days of childhood I would poke one leaf through another to make a boat with a sail. I would use the bigger ones as fans on a hot day, or tear them into tiny pieces for ants to take away. All of which probably helped me appreciate these words by our prolific but elusive friend "Ann Onymous."

"Anyone can love a rose but it takes a lot to love a leaf. It's ordinary to love the beautiful, but it's beautiful to love the ordinary."

Now, in days of adulthood, I understand the same appreciation applies to people as well, and have found many ordinary lives to be amongst the most beautiful.

ONE of the most delightful places in the Channel Islands is the beautiful island of Sark. For the many tourists arriving in the summer, the prospect of peace and quiet and relaxation is most welcome.

For the locals, whatever the season, they have the joy of their "dark skies".

This is how they describe the wonder of the heavens and the delight of stargazing.

"There are no street lights on Sark and no traffic and therefore nothing to detract from the beauty of the night sky."

The rest of us may not be so fortunate, but on a clear night, if we can take a little time for stargazing, even from our bedroom windows, we may manage to capture something of the peace and serenity found on Sark.

I know I always feel much better for it, and I hope you will, too.

Tuesday — July 19

JEANNIE was having one of those days.

"First, I broke my favourite mug," she told me. "Then I left my umbrella on the bus, and when I finally got home, wet through, it took me ten minutes to find my door key. Oh, well, I'm sure tomorrow will be better!"

I'm pretty sure it will, for happily Jeannie is not the sort of person to be defeated by events. Indeed, she is a water-colour artist of some repute who, over the years, has had to overcome far more challenging problems, including illness and many rejections, in order to achieve her present successful career.

It was Henry Ford who said, "When everything seems to be going against you, remember that the airplane takes off against the wind – not with it."

I hope that, whatever our dreams may be, we can all take heart from those words.

With courage, who knows how high we may fly!

Wednesday — July 20

REGRETS can flit through every life,
From large to much more slight,
Like: "Wish I'd not had all those cakes,
Or stayed out late last night."
Such idle thoughts are hardly worth
A moment's feeling blue,
For all the things that haunt us most
Are things we didn't do.
So don't let chances slip away,
Just seize the day, and fly!
Regrets come not from what we've done,
But all we've let slip by.

– Margaret Ingall.

Thursday — July 21

WHEN you were at school, did the teacher ever give out 100 lines for some misdemeanour? Errant pupils were made to write 100 times, "I must . . . (or must not . . .)" do whatever the misbehaviour was. Today I am going to try to write 100 lines for myself, to remind me of my life's ethos, starting with – "I must be more thankful"; "I must attend to the needs of others"; "I must not take my friends for granted"; and try to reach 100.

Why don't you try this, too?

Friday — July 22

IT'S interesting to note that Erich Fried first found fame in Germany through his political poetry, but later in life he focused more on verses of love; almost as if his passion, or his priority, had moved a foot or so south, from his head to his heart.

It's a notion he himself tackles in one of his works where he tries to teach his head that "a good heart is more use as a brain."

What would the world be like, I wonder, if we moved more of our thinking a foot or so south?

Saturday — July 23

I READ about two girls who went walking along a beach that was more pebbles than sand. They took permanent markers with them and drew smiley faces, or love-hearts, or wrote little uplifting messages like "Love Wins," on pebbles as they walked.

Some time later they found that someone had photographed a couple of the stones and posted them on a website. Their pebbles, and their messages, were famous.

It occurred to me that anyone with a sharp eye would be able to tell where the girls began walking, where they went, and where they left the beach, by following their decorated pebbles.

And I thought, "Wouldn't that be a wonderful way to live a life – so that, after we are gone, people would know where we had been by the trail of love and smiles we left behind?"

Sunday — July 24

THE clergyman and poet Andrew Young was also a bit of a botanist. But he never collected flowers. Instead, he stored up images of them in his memory. In the same way he is said to have "collected" barns, churches, villages, mountains and streams.

All at no expense and with no specialist equipment, or title deeds, required.

Which made me wonder – would a collection of things which existed both in their original location and in your memory best be called a re-collection?

Monday — July 25

WHEN was the last time you changed some aspect of your life? Change is inevitable, though many people fear it. If you are struggling with a situation you are afraid of, ask yourself what exactly it is that you fear. Then face up to it and alter the situation. You'll find that the change was not as daunting as you first thought – it might even be the best thing you ever did!

Tuesday — July 26

SHIRLEY was in her garden when I called round to drop off some magazines.

"Come and have a cup of tea with me," she invited. "I'm just sitting on the bench enjoying the sunshine and the peace. And what's more, I'm refusing to feel at all guilty about it."

Three cheers for Shirley! It's so easy to fall into the trap of feeling we ought to fill every hour busily, that we ignore the really important business of simply enjoying the loveliness of the world.

It was writer George MacDonald who pointed out, "Work is not always required. There is such a thing as sacred idleness – the cultivation of which is now fearfully neglected."

And that really would be something to feel guilty about!

Wednesday — July 27

THERE'S a school of thought that suggests great achievements often come from some inner turmoil and, looking at some of the troubled geniuses who have benefited mankind, I would have to say there is some truth in it.

But when a twenty-year-old boy from the town of Vinci became a member of the Guild of Artists he drew a sketch of the Arno valley and wrote across the back of the canvas, *Sono contenti* or *I am happy*. And, of course, Leonardo da Vinci's greatest works, including the Mona Lisa and the Last Supper, were yet to come.

If a discontented mind is supposed to be fertile ground for innovation then how much more fruitful must a happy heart be?

Thursday — July 28

NOBEL Prize winner Odysseas Elytis once wrote, "You'll come to learn a great deal if you study the insignificant in depth."

I should say so. Like the comforting fact that absolutely nothing is insignificant; that everything and each of us has a purpose and an important role to play.

Friday — July 29

WHEN we are young we just know we are going to change the world! Alas, it's only as we grow older that we realise it's actually not quite so simple . . . And yet I suspect that many of us do change things more than we realise.

This quote from American minister and educator Fred Rogers certainly made me think. He said, "If you could only sense how important you are to the lives of those you meet; how important you can be to the people you may never even dream of. There is something of yourself that you leave at every meeting with another person."

Which made me reflect on all the various quotations I've shared with you over the years. I'm sure that very few of those people ever dreamed that their words would live on to enrich and inspire us – and yet they do.

So never be tempted to believe that your contribution to the world is insignificant. Your influence may be greater than you realise!

Saturday — July 30

TEARS of joy are an odd concept. But it's a fact that we cry when we are deeply happy. So, is there any difference between the two kinds of tears? I like the description offered by 18th-century clergyman Hosea Ballou.

"Tears of joy," he wrote, "are like the summer rain drops pierced by sunbeams."

And the other kind? Well, they are a challenge to each of us to create more joy and give people better reasons to cry.

Sunday — July 31

THERE is an old Russian proverb that says, "Every day is a messenger of God."

A simple enough saying. Imagine if we took it seriously and began each day by listening to that message, then ended each day with our reply.

August

Monday — August 1

THE garden centre must have seemed a strange place to the bee, with all those tamed, shaped and potted plants, but it carried on regardless, collecting pollen just as it would have in the wild.

A verse by the 18th century painter William Hogarth might have been written for that bee – and any of us who find ourselves in confusing situations.

"To Nature and Yourself appeal,

Nor learn of others what to feel."

Stay true to your heart and your God-given nature, no matter the circumstance, and the product of your day's labour should be as sweet as the bee's.

Tuesday — August 2

DOUBTLESS the checkout operator expected a cuter answer. The mum was loading shopping on to the conveyor belt while the four-year-old held the pram with a baby in it.

"Oh," she said, "are you looking after your little sister?"

"Yes," the girl said. "It's a full-time job and I'm fed up with it!"

Mum rolled her eyes. She and the checkout operator exchanged understanding smiles.

The girl obviously felt the weight of the world was on her shoulders. Whatever her imagined burdens, her mother was behind her taking care of the important stuff.

We can laugh, but which of us hasn't felt over-burdened? Which of us hasn't depended on our own strength and found it lacking? Just know that, while we are huffing and puffing, God, like that mother, is right there with us, actually bearing the weight of the world.

No doubt He rolls his eyes and smiles an understanding smile from time to time.

Bee Happy!

Wednesday — August 3

VIRTUE brings its own reward." It's a bit of an ambiguous phrase; perhaps even a warning that we really shouldn't expect any other kind of benefit.

But happily, as Scottish journalist C.B. Forbes pointed out, there is at least one good quality which brings its own very definite reward.

He said, "Cheerfulness is among the most laudable virtues. It gains you the good will and friendship of others. It blesses those who practise it and those upon whom it is bestowed."

And I can't think of a better payment than that!

Thursday — August 4

MY sweetheart and I were in a fish 'n' chip cafe. There were two old ladies at the next table and one of them laughed at something the other said.

"When you laugh," her friend observed, "you REALLY laugh."

The other lady said, "I'm ninety and I don't have time left to waste on unimportant stuff. So I'm going to put my heart and soul into the important things while I can."

I'd like to suggest we don't have to be ninety for that to apply. And, as life-lessons go, I think it's one we would all have a laugh learning.

Friday — August 5

NOW, hands up – who would like to be a work of art?

I suspect if we are honest, most of us would be rather pleased to be regarded in that light!

But poet Anita Krizzan is in no doubt that we are already. She said, "We are mosaics. Pieces of light, love, history, stars . . . glued together with magic and music and words."

What a glorious way to describe a human being and, better still, it's totally true of each one of us.

Saturday — August 6

WHICH would you think the longest? The road between Portsmouth and Glasgow, or the road from Manchester to Leeds, or the road from London (via the Channel Tunnel) to Paris? Judged strictly in miles there is, of course, a first, second and third – but I haven't even stopped to think what they might be.

You see, according to an old Turkish proverb, it depends on more than the miles. It depends on who you are travelling with. And that's what I wanted to emphasise.

"No road is long," they say, "when travelling in good company."

Sunday — August 7

WHEN we take time at bedtime to think about how the day went, what kind of questions do we ask? How did work go? Was there anything worth watching on the television?

All valid questions, to be sure. But the theologian and writer Henri Nouwen had some other suggestions; ones we might adopt for the betterment of our days and the days of those around us.

"Did I offer peace today?
Did I bring a smile to someone's face?
Did I say words of healing?
Did I forgive?
Did I love?"

Monday — August 8

NOMADIC peoples learn to depend on each other. So much so that I hear the Penan people of Borneo actually have no words in their language for thank you. Everything is shared as a matter of course.

We might follow that example – to a point – giving whatever we have without any expectation of thanks. But when we receive we can add to the gift by sharing our gratitude. After all, we do have "thank you" in our language and it would be a shame not to use it to best effect.

Tuesday — August 9

THE visit to the food bank must have been an eye-opener for the secondary school group. They were in uniform, young, healthy, transported there and collected again at the end. They had places to sleep and were guaranteed meals. They must have felt they had nothing in common with the people collecting food parcels.

Towards the end of their visit I asked what they thought of it all.

"It's a lesson in how communities help themselves," a girl said, "and it might be the most important lesson we ever learn!"

On their way out every one of them voluntarily dropped money in the donations box.

Bless their hearts, I'd say the lesson has been well learned!

Wednesday — August 10

THE Lady of the House and I were flying on holiday one year when we were delayed at the airport for a few hours. We decided to head off for a cup of tea. I got chatting to an elderly lady who was also delayed and who was enjoying a scone and jam.

"I don't normally eat sweet things," she confided, "but I'm on holiday and I have been since I left the house. I can go back to being good when I get home in a week's time!"

We joined her and ordered two pastries ourselves. Sometimes you just need to treat yourself, whether you are on holiday or not. It's those little pleasures that make life worth living!

Thursday — August 11

WRITERS often draw inspiration from the things they see around them and share it with the world through their work. But playwright Tennessee Williams thought it applied to everyone.

"We are all here to bear witness to something," he wrote, "to be of some aid and direction to other people."

Let's hope the story we bear witness to – and reflect in our life – provides useful aid and good direction to all who see our "play".

Friday — August 12

BILL is as fond of finding inspirational sayings as I am, so we are often in friendly competition to see who can come up with the best.

On this occasion, I had to concede to Bill, for although I've heard life compared to many things, the following words from Marion Howard do put it in very human terms: "Life is like a blanket that's too short. You pull it up and your toes rebel, you yank it down and shivers meander about your shoulder; but cheerful folks manage to draw their knees up and pass a very comfortable night."

Yes, indeed!

Saturday — August 13

FAR be it from me to argue with ancient wisdom, but I had to shake my head when I read the proverb, "An onion shared with a friend tastes like roast lamb."

Noticing my expression, the Lady of the House asked what was annoying me, so I repeated the proverb to her, expecting her to join in my disagreement.

"Hmm," she said thoughtfully. "Perhaps it's the friendship that adds the flavour to the meal."

Far be it from me to disagree with wifely wisdom!

Sunday — August 14

SUNDAY is my quiet day,
A day to pause, to rest,
To stop, and in the silence,
To dwell on all that's best.
I love this Sunday stillness,
Most blest of all the days,
May always we have Sundays
For peace and joy and praise.

– Margaret Ingall.

Monday — August 15

I WAS reading "Alice's Adventures In Wonderland" to my great-niece whilst on babysitting duty when I came across these words – "She generally gave herself very good advice (though she very seldom followed it)."

It's something I am sure we all do and for a moment I lost myself in consideration of a world where we all followed the advice of our better selves.

It was only for a moment, and my advice to other babysitters (if they don't want to be thought too strange) is to keep reading, do all the voices, and save the philosophy for less important times.

Tuesday — August 16

JUNE, the choir mistress, doesn't beat about the bush. Despairing of the choir's efforts, she put her music down and asked, "Does anyone know what the word 'amateur' means?"

I was surprised. Surely she wasn't going to insult the whole choir! Then she explained.

"It comes from the Latin 'amator', or 'lover'. It means someone who does a thing for the love of it. That's how I want you to sing. Like you love doing it! If you look like you love what you're doing, your audience are more likely to love it as well."

Faces brightened considerably as the choir realised they did, in fact, love what they were doing and they could, in fact, show it!

And those of us who can't sing can apply the same advice to how we live our lives. Live it like you love it!

Wednesday — August 17

I RECENTLY had occasion to visit a friend in his place of work. On the wall above his desk was what people now call an inspirational poster.

It read: "Life works best when we do."

A good thought for employees and bosses alike, wouldn't you say?

Thursday — August 18

*O*H, how we curse nettles when gardening,
Their pretty leaves covered in stings,
Half an inch of bare skin – they will find it!
We list them with Nature's worst things.

Yet their young shoots are bright and nutritious
And our animals find them a treat,
Their stems can make fibre, their leaves produce dye
And their soup is delicious to eat.

A large swathe of nettles left growing
Serves the butterfly laying her eggs,
And as long as some patches of docks are nearby
We can rub them on stung arms and legs.

For all things in life have a purpose,
We must look for the positives there
And trust that the Lord has his reasons,
But find thicker gloves we can wear!

– Eliza Barret.

Friday — August 19

THE man walked back into his living-room, ignoring the fact that his annoyed wife was also ignoring him. He walked to the front window, the back window, the fireplace and finally to the couch where she sat.

He knelt down, picked up the slipper that had fallen unnoticed from her foot, and said, "I have searched the four corners of my kingdom for my one true love. The slipper fits. It must be you!"

And all thoughts of their argument flew from her mind.

It's worth remembering that marriage has its difficulties, but the possibility of a happy ever after is always in our hands – or on our feet – if we have the heart to make it so!

Saturday — August 20

HARRY'S always been an active sort of fellow, so I was surprised when he told me he had started exercising and was feeling the good of it.

"Push ups," I suggested, raising a quizzical eyebrow. "Jogging? Weights?"

"None of those!" He dismissed my comments with a laugh. "I'm exercising discretion, in what I say and who I say it to. I feel much better for the lack of arguments and misunderstandings in my life."

Well! I should just be glad he told me about it, really.

Sunday — August 21

A TATTERED old book on my shelf of favourites describes itself as "A thought – a recipe – a household hint – for every day of the year." And it has all of those things. But inside the cover are a few words which it calls "One thought, for the morning of every day of every year."

What are those words?

"I will make this day worthwhile – for someone else!"

A wonderful challenge to the reader and as valid today as it was when the book was compiled in 1936.

Monday — August 22

WALK to what you're scared of,
I wonder if you dare?
For often it's not easy
To face your fear foursquare,
And yet if you can do so
With courage, not despair,
When finally you reach it –
You'll find there's nothing there.

– Margaret Ingall.

Tuesday — August 23

DESPITE not having mentioned it to anyone, our dear friend Mary still managed to get a fair collection of gifts for her birthday. I had stopped by with the offer of posting her thank-you cards and she handed them to me with a deeply contented sigh.

"You know," she said, "I get as much pleasure from the thank-yous as I do from the gifts."

Her obvious happiness reminded me of something a friend had said years before.

"Once you realise that gratitude is a gift in itself," he told me, "the whole world seems to come already wrapped in ribbons and bows."

Wednesday — August 24

HAVE you ever worked a miracle?

I'm imagining you don't think so, but Dag Hammarskjöld, who used to be Secretary-General of the United Nations, would probably have disagreed with you. He wasn't talking about show-stopping stuff like parting the sea or walking on water. He had in mind something all of us can do.

"Forgiveness," he wrote, "is the answer to a child's dream of a miracle, by which what is broken is made whole again."

May your life be one of many miracles.

Thursday — August 25

DO you know what a rangoli is? It's a design drawn in ground corn outside Indian homes to symbolise welcome. They can be very colourful and amazingly intricate but, of course, little creatures eat them, the wind blows them and the feet of those being welcomed will wear them away.

We all have different ways of making people feel welcome, but if the rangoli teaches us anything it is this – our hospitality should constantly be refreshed and renewed and out front for everyone to see.

Friday — August 26

I'M afraid I definitely wasn't a model teenager," Pippa admitted. "I left school early and with no idea what I wanted to do. But even though I had nothing better to occupy me, I still wasn't pleased to find my parents had volunteered me to help an elderly neighbour decorate her front room. But not only was my neighbour grateful for help, she also encouraged me to come up with my own ideas of decor. It was so rewarding that I went back to college to learn more, and now I'm a full-time interior design consultant."

And her talents are much sought after, too! As Mahatma Gandhi observed, "The best way to find yourself is to lose yourself in the service of others."

Saturday — August 27

WE might talk of "holding a grudge", but more often the phrase used is "bearing a grudge". Bearing means carrying and a grudge against someone, particularly a friend or family member, can be a heavy load to carry.

Do yourself (as much as the other person) a favour, drop that grudge. It will lighten your load, and your heart.

Sunday — August 28

THERE'S a tale of a bishop in olden days who went to visit a desert-dwelling monk noted for his piety. The bishop's men begged the monk to speak to him that he might learn.

The monk replied, "If he cannot learn from my silence, he will not learn from my words."

A strange thing to say? Well, some people are a little too fond of talking. The monk, who was obviously not under any vow of silence, probably preferred to be doing.

The lesson was not in whatever he might have had to say, but in how he lived his life. Example is always the best teacher. And the best way to preach a sermon is to live it.

Monday — August 29

READING up on the Japanese tea ceremony, I commented to the Lady of the House that it was traditional to compliment the home or the ornaments in the room belonging to the person who was serving the tea.

"Oh, I always do that anyway," my sweetheart replied.

"Why on earth would you bother?" the philistine in me asked.

"Because, if the people are interesting, and they almost always are, then the ornaments they surround themselves with will usually have an interesting story behind them."

People and their ornaments; both, it seems, well worth considering over a cup of tea!

Tuesday — August 30

I CAN'T believe he would think this, but the inventor and artist Leonardo da Vinci once said, "I have offended God and mankind because my work didn't reach the quality it should have."

Surely not! But it did encourage me to wonder what heights the rest of us might reach if we, too, felt we owed God and mankind nothing but our very best.

Wednesday — August 31

IT'S difficult to imagine any life that doesn't have some kind of impact. I'm not sure there actually is such a thing. Even if you don't write books, or start campaigns, or ever become famous, think of the people you meet each day and what they take away from those encounters. Think of the little kindnesses you give (or withhold.) Think of the example you set, even to the people you pass in the street.

Jane Goodall made her fame as a conservationist, working with chimpanzees and gorillas in Tanzania, but her words might apply equally to those of us who never ventured as far.

"What you do makes a difference," she wrote. "You have to decide what kind of difference you want to make."

September

Thursday — September 1

SIMON had just attended his graduation ceremony after three hard-working years at university. During family celebrations, talk turned to what might be considered the hardest test they'd ever encountered.

"School maths test," young Sam insisted.

"No – the driving test," his mum said, while the rival claims of all kinds of trials soon followed thick and fast.

But it was Grandad who had the last word.

"I agree with the words of an Indian philosopher called Sri Chinmoy," he said. "It was his opinion that 'To be true to oneself is the hardest test of life'. In my experience he's entirely right."

I think so, too. But oh, the satisfaction if you can manage to pass that one!

Friday — September 2

IF you could choose – where would you live?

I don't imagine that many of us would have to think too long for an answer, for who has never dreamed of that cottage in the country, the rambling house overlooking the sea, or perhaps even a smart flat in the middle of the city?

Well, if you are sadly sighing that you don't have the ability to choose, take heart, for the most important part of the decision is certainly within our choice.

It was Lao Tzu who said, "If you are depressed you are living in the past. If you are anxious you are living in the future. If you are at peace you are living in the present."

Welcome to the best residence in the world!

Saturday — September 3

FRIENDS of ours work in a support capacity with people from all around the world. Every once in a while they will invite people to their house for a little respite. Now, they are a family of seven and their house already seems full to capacity.

When I heard they had a family of four coming to stay with them I couldn't begin to imagine how everyone would fit in.

"Ah," my friend said, "there's an old Danish proverb that helps us at times like this. 'When there is room in the heart, there is room in the house'."

He does have a big heart, my friend!

Sunday — September 4

THE author Henri Nouwen once interviewed a pair of trapeze artists. They explained the very special relationship that exists between the flyer and the catcher. One has to be prepared to let go and the other has to be prepared to bring their partner to safety.

But the one thing the flyer must never do is try to catch the catcher! That way, apparently, lies disaster. Only one of them does the catching and, until that happens, the other must concentrate on one thing only – flying!

At times, when we are stressed or worried, we might be tempted to hurry God along, or try to do His work for Him. But we need to trust that He won't let us fall. He's the catcher. That's His job. And, until then, it's our job to keep flying!

Monday — September 5

THEY say the greatest speeches in history have all been short ones. I can't imagine, however, that any of the authors of those speeches could cram as much truth, philosophy and impact into five words as whoever wrote these five words on a church noticeboard – "Give love. Receive love."

And the fifth word?

"Repeat."

Tuesday — September 6

EVERYTHING happens for a reason,
Or so the proverbs say,
Sometimes that's hard to understand
When things don't go our way.
The reason may be quite obscure
And part of life's rich plan,
But we must strive and hope and dream
And do the best we can.
So keep on stepping forward
And hold your head up high,
Whatever reason there may be
We'll find out, by and by.

– Iris Hesselden.

Wednesday — September 7

TO win Nobel prizes in chemistry and physics Marie Curie must have spent an awful lot of time in the laboratory, and there are plenty of photos showing her, test tube in hand, experimenting on something or other. But her non-scientific notes describe her love of the outdoors, especially in spring.

"All my life through," she wrote, "the new sights of nature made me rejoice like a child."

Marie Curie identified two new elements, a feat I doubt many of us will emulate. She must have been excited then. But it was the wonders of nature that made her "rejoice like a child" – and we can all share in those discoveries.

Thursday — September 8

DO you know people who go out of their way to do deeds and achieve things purely to gain some publicity or respect? I thought about it, and surely it is better to earn respect without getting it, than to get respect without earning it? A thought to consider for today and every day.

Friday — September 9

THE Lady of the House and I were watching a re-run of the old classic "Ben-Hur".

I couldn't help regretting I had never had the chance to be a charioteer. It looked thrilling!

"Oh, we each of us have that chance," my good lady said. She smiled at my obvious confusion then added, "With our emotions. They can be like powerful horses at times. We can tame them and use their energy to win the race. Or we can let them run wild, in which case you never know where you might end up."

I said nothing, lost in admiration at her ability to draw a life-lesson from an old film, and glad, as always, to have her as co-driver in the chariot of our life.

Saturday — September 10

PEOPLE have played music on all kinds of "instruments," from polished brass trumpets to galvanised dust-bin lids, from a silver-keyed piccolo to a drilled-out carrot. But . . . on a life? The art critic, painter and philanthropist John Ruskin believed it was possible.

"All one's life is music," he wrote, "if we touch the notes rightly and in time."

The question is, can you be bothered to learn how to play the music of your life? And a better question might be, would you like it to sound like a beautiful symphony – or a carrot with holes in it?

Sunday — September 11

AFTER the Great Fire of London destroyed his sorting office, the Post Master General James Hicks relocated with as much mail as he could salvage. Once out of danger he wrote to all his colleagues, letting them know where to find him and making arrangements for the continuation of the postal service. He wrote, "I am in ye Red Lyon in Barnet with my family & God." Despite losses and suffering, Mr Hicks routinely assumed he was in God's company, wherever he might be. Just as we can.

Monday — September 12

HAVING clothed every extremity in wool and water-proofing as defence against the weather I saw out the window, I strode out to find – it wasn't all that bad!

E.B. White, the author of "Charlotte's Web", once quoted a sailor's maxim that summed the situation up perfectly. "The weather," he wrote, "is a great bluffer!"

And the same goes for all kinds of unpleasant situations. You might find them dreadful in anticipation, but they will be much more manageable once you call their bluff!

Tuesday — September 13

I HAD the pleasure of reading the story of Walt Disney's "Dumbo" to some attentive little listeners recently. Dumbo and I got a round of applause at the end, and I also got some food for thought.

After all his hardships and indignities Dumbo flaps his enormous ears and learns to fly. He becomes famous. His mother is released and gets a pension, the circus is named after him, he travels across America in his own luxury train. But best of all . . .

Best of all? Could it get better? Yes. Best of all . . . he forgives everyone who had ever been unkind to him!

May my little listeners have ears to hear and hearts to remember!

Wednesday — September 14

THERE is a part of human nature that drives some of us towards making a big impact. We want to be noticed. We want to make a difference. We want to do something big!

And, all too often, the art of doing little things gets overlooked.

Which is why I like to share these words on the subject by Saint Thérèse of Lisieux.

"Miss no opportunity of making some small sacrifice; here by a smiling look, there by a kindly word; always doing the smallest thing right – and doing it all for love."

Thursday — September 15

HAVE you ever gazed out to sea and lost yourself in wonder? Why? Has anyone ever done a good deed for you and left you wondering why they would do such a thing?

Have you ever in your life found yourself happy or contented for no particular reason?

One Russian pianist, composer and conductor probably felt the same about music.

"I have never understood a bar of music in my life," he said, "but I have felt it!"

There is so much that is good and uplifting in this world that is beyond understanding, that can only be felt – which means that even dullards like me can enjoy it!

Friday — September 16

THE film director Jean-Luc Godard liked to shake things up a little. "A story should have a beginning, a middle, and an end," he once said. "But not necessarily in that order."

He would surely appreciate the wonderful story that is each of our lives. They all have middles and ends – but they can have as many beginnings as we have the heart and imagination for!

Saturday — September 17

I DIDN'T choose the greetings card for the colour or design. In fact, there is no colour, simply black lettering on a white background. However, it now has a place of honour on my desk and I look at it every day. These are the words: "Everything happens for a reason."

Not quite so easy to accept, is it?

And yet if we look back on our lives, there are many pieces which, like a jigsaw, fit together as they should.

It's not always up to us to reason why, but just to try hard to accept whatever life brings our way.

Sunday — September 18

STEPHANIE is part of a project that helps street-children and orphans in Romania.

Teaching them about the weather and the seasons as part of their schooling, she asked if anyone could tell her what was shining down on them today.

A little girl raised her hand and answered, "Cer!"

Stephanie had meant the sun, which would have been "soare" in Romanian. But "Cer", as well as meaning "sky", also means "heaven" or "the heavens."

"If the only thing I teach them," Stephanie told me, "is that heaven shines down on them, regardless of the weather or the season, then I will count my work as well done."

Monday — September 19

SMILING faces and Monday mornings don't always go together, so I was pleasantly surprised to see a big cheerful grin on my neighbour Anne's face.

"Ah, but I've got a present waiting for me," she explained.

"A nice one?" I had to ask.

She laughed.

"I don't know yet. You see, I'm trusting in the words of Horace, the Roman poet. He said, 'Cease to inquire what the future has in store, and take as a gift whatever the day brings forth.' So that's just what I'm going to do."

Now that's an excellent thought for any morning!

Tuesday — September 20

ALEXANDER DUMAS THE YOUNGER was a successful playwright who had a view on friendship his father's Three Musketeers might have given a hearty cheer for.

"Friendship," he wrote, "consists of forgetting what one gives – and remembering what one receives."

SURROUNDED – as we often are – by noise,
One may forget that one of life's great joys
Lies in the blissful state of solitude,
In which we have the freedom to exclude
The most unpleasant trespassers, and find
Uncharted peaceful regions of our mind.
Desirable as lots of friends may be,
Each hour of solitude is ecstasy.

– Dennis W. Turner.

Thursday — September 22

I'VE often heard it said that breakfast should set you up for the rest of the day," Alfred announced with satisfaction, "and this morning it certainly did."

Well – I had to ask more! It appears that on two Sundays each year the residents of Alfred's village get together to hold a Big Breakfast in the community hall. Lots of ingredients are donated, and as many as possible are produced locally, ranging from muesli and sausages to toast and jam. All money raised goes towards village projects.

"But best of all," said Alfred, "it's the perfect way to catch up with friends and neighbours – and even meet a few strangers."

Mmm. Now, that does sound like an appetising idea!

Friday — September 23

I'M sure we all admire those people who "rise to the occasion." The country might need a leader, a friend might be in need, an example might need set and some brave soul rises to the occasion.

But what of the rest of us? Could we be like that? Maybe if the circumstances were right. Or we could take the circumstances as they are and still make a difference for the better.

As Dustin Hoffman's character in "Mr Magorium's Wonder Emporium" said, "Your life is an occasion. Rise to it."

Saturday — September 24

I AM sure the world has seasons for better reason than to delight children, but there's no doubting that they do. Which of us, having made daisy chains, kicked through mounds of rustling leaves and skated on frozen puddles would not call ourselves much blessed?

Robert Louis Stevenson once wrote of the pleasures children find in the different seasons.

"To make this earth our hermitage

A cheerful and changeful place,

God's bright and intricate device

Of days and seasons doth suffice."

Sunday — September 25

THE man was one of four or five who were sailing boats across the park pond. The gold lettering along the side of a scale-model clipper made it stand out from the rest. I managed to be by the side of its "Captain" as he brought it to shore. The motto read, "The man who walks with God always gets to his destination."

"True?" I queried.

"Of course," he insisted. "The destination of the man who walks with God is God. So, the place he hopes to get to will always be right beside Him."

True through storms and calm seas.

Monday — September 26

I WAS becoming so wound up about things," Ellen confided, "that I can't tell you how grateful I was to have friends around!"

Ellen was talking about her recent house move, but I imagine there are few of us who have never been stressed by having to deal with difficult circumstances. It's then that we can be glad of friends. Thomas Chandler said, "To love a person is to learn the song that is in their heart, and to sing it to them when they have forgotten."

Let us thank God for those who help us to remember.

Tuesday — September 27

YOU know, I'm sometimes surprised," Katie said, "just how often the very people who are kindest to others are the same ones who are hardest upon themselves."

She had been telling me of her friend, a wonderfully warm and caring lady who, despite raising a substantial amount for her favourite charity, had been thoroughly downcast to not quite achieve the full target she'd set for herself.

She somehow felt she had let the charity down, though they, of course, were thrilled with any donation.

"So I told her of one of my favourite quotes," Katie said. "It was the Dalai Lama who pointed out that, 'If you want others to be happy, practise compassion. If you want to be happy, practise compassion'."

That's a great thought, and I do hope Katie's friend takes note. In fact, come to think of it, perhaps we should all take note!

Wednesday — September 28

NOW, here's a question for you – when you go to bed each night, do you drift sweetly into peaceful sleep – or lie awake worrying about all that's gone wrong with the day?

Well, I suspect we all give way to the latter from time to time, especially if there's a particular situation we feel we could have handled better.

That's when I like to take the advice of that wise man Ralph Waldo Emerson. He counselled thus.

"Finish each day and be done with it. You have done what you could. Some blunders and absurdities no doubt crept in; forget them as soon as you can. Tomorrow is a new day. You shall begin it serenely and with too high a spirit to be encumbered with your old nonsense."

I like his use of the word "nonsense", for so often that is exactly what it all is.

Sleep well!

Thursday — September 29

"KEEP close to Nature's heart . . . break away once in a while, and climb a mountain or spend a week in the woods. Wash your spirit clean."

That excellent piece of advice comes from the naturalist John Muir, but I can almost hear you thinking – yes, it's a lovely thought, but not entirely practical!

Well, we'll agree to spare ourselves the mountain and the woods, but that doesn't mean we can't adapt the idea. Happily, a day in the countryside, or even a short stroll round the park, is much more achievable, and equally as good for our spirits.

As John Muir would agree, Nature's heart is generous, and even the briefest encounter can't help but make us feel better.

Friday — September 30

TODAY I have nowhere to go,
I don't need to be here or be there,
I've a wonderful feeling of space,
For today I'm as free as the air.

Today I can sit in the window
And watch as the world hurries by,
Or curl up with a book by the fireside,
And no-one is going to ask why.

I could sit and eat biscuits all day,
Or invite a friend round for some tea,
And I won't feel a moment of guilt, because
I'm completely and utterly free.

Today I can watch the rain fall,
Or the flowers and trees as they grow,
I can do just whatever I want,
For today I have nowhere to go!

– Eliza Barret.

October

Saturday — October 1

AS the trees gently lay their insulating blanket of leaves over the earth again I am reminded of how much the writer George Eliot loved this time of year.

"Delicious autumn," she once wrote, "my very soul is wedded to it, and if I were a bird I would fly about the earth seeking the successive autumns."

A beautiful thought. But, personally, I enjoy all of the seasons. I think four is just enough variety for a year and I'm glad we don't have to go in search of them. If we stay where we are they will come to us, lining up in an orderly fashion just to bring their unique challenges and delights to us!

Sunday — October 2

WHAT does friendship really mean?
It's being generous and kind;
A compliment, a listening ear,
It's others' feelings kept in mind.
A smile or a much-needed hug,
A gentle squeeze of someone's hand,
A card to say they're in your thoughts,
Or words to show you understand.
A thoughtful gift, a special treat,
Support, respect and empathy;
Remembering important days
And showing trust and loyalty.
It's all these things and many more,
That's what a lasting friendship brings.
So, what is friendship? Nothing big,
But just a thousand tiny things.

– Emma Canning.

Monday — October 3

P RAYER!" he said. "It's great when you are talking to God and asking for help with your stuff. But what about when you're the guy He chooses to use to make someone else's prayer come true? And you don't want to. That's when it becomes a bit more difficult."

"So, what did you do?" I asked.

"Well, I did it, didn't I? It's God that's asking, isn't it? But that doesn't mean I have to be happy about it."

Doesn't it, I wondered as I walked away. I agreed it was an awkward position to be in, and an aspect of prayer we don't often think about, but . . . being happy about it . . . maybe that's something worth working on.

Tuesday — October 4

W HEN I was young, my great-aunt Ellen lived just down the road," Frank said. "But I'm afraid we children were never that keen to visit, for she was the sort of person quite unable to see the lighter side of anything."

I suppose a fit of the grumbles and glooms can attack all of us from time to time, but to allow it to become a habit is never a good thing.

That's why I like the words of Indian writer Ritu Ghatourey: "Don't let yourself be a victim of your negative thoughts. They're just thoughts, not reality. Don't let them destroy you."

And if you can manage that, you will be a victor in all sorts of ways.

Wednesday — October 5

T HE book of Matthew, chapter 3 verse 2 reads: "Repent ye, for the kingdom of Heaven is at hand".

Repentance means to change your attitude about God, which will in turn alter your habits, decisions and deeds. Put simply, repentance is detesting sin enough to reject it completely.

Perhaps we could all consider this quietly when the temptation of sin is within us.

Thursday — October 6

"YOU'VE heard the old saying, 'Strong fences make good neighbours,' Francis."

I agreed with Harry that I had.

"Well, it's usually meant as keeping them on their side and you on yours, protecting what you have from others."

Again I agreed.

"But come look at this," he said, directing me to a cardboard "plaque" on his brand-new fence. It read, "In memory of Old Fence, where many a gardening tip was shared, over which children were passed for babysitting and food for sampling. It supported us when we leaned on it, chatting hours away. Gone but always appreciated."

Fences needn't be separating barriers. They can often be the meeting place where neighbours become friends.

Friday — October 7

WHEN one angler wishes another "Fisherman's luck" it means "good luck" but with the understanding that even the best of them has to be content with whatever he catches (or doesn't catch) on the day. But that doesn't mean it's all down to chance.

In his 1899 book named after the phrase Henry van Dyke wrote, "When I talk of fisherman's luck I do not forget there are deeper things behind it. I remember that what we call our fortunes, good or ill, are but the wise dealings and distributions of a Wisdom higher and a Kindness greater than our own."

Saturday — October 8

HAVE you ever wished that you could do a bit more good in the world – but unfortunately the opportunity never seems to arise? Then perhaps you have not been looking hard enough. It was the Roman philosopher Seneca who said, "Wherever there is a human being, there is an opportunity for kindness."

Which means that if you just happen to be a human being who is reading this, then the chance could be right on your doorstep!

Sunday — October 9

HAVE you ever attended a meeting of Friends? I don't mean mates and pals. The Society of Friends are more popularly known as the Quakers. Some of their meetings are held in silent contemplation, seeking to hear that quiet inner voice they believe comes from above.

It's a habit worth trying. And when you do hear – and get used to – that voice, the voice of God, you will find that He is a friend, too.

Monday — October 10

KATE was at the garden centre.

"I've made up my mind at last." She smiled. "For ages I've been wanting a holly tree, but telling myself it's silly when I know it's such a slow grower, and won't reach maturity for years. Then I happened to mention my dilemma to a friend. She laughed and told me that if that was the case then I'd better plant one this afternoon!"

What a wise friend – and what a lesson to be learned. Sometimes we just need to stop worrying about tomorrow, and get on with it!

Tuesday — October 11

WHEN Jack was born his mother was told he might not live and if he did he would never amount to anything.

When he was eight someone persuaded his mum to let him run in a race where the kids collected beanbags as they ran. As she watched him trail the pack, hobbling in his callipers, she vowed never to embarrass him like that again – until she saw all the beanbags in his basket.

Excitedly, he told her the other kids had been running so fast that lots of beanbags had fallen from their baskets. He'd been going slowly enough to gather them all up.

Jack went on to become a successful doctor.

Sometimes you win the race just by taking part!

Wednesday — October 12

HARVEST time! Whose heart doesn't rise at the sight of trees dripping with fruit, the gardens full of vegetables, and the shops and markets rich and colourful with all the produce of this time of year. But what yields the best crop? Well, I may be drifting a little from the subject, but when I think of all nature's gifts I can't help thinking of a quotation from Abraham Lincoln, who said, "I have always found that mercy bears richer fruits than strict justice."

Admittedly not edible, but still full of sweetness!

Thursday — October 13

ENID is a campaigner. Not a militant one, you understand, but the sort of quietly persistent person who, when a playground is threatened with closure or a busy road needs a pedestrian crossing, quietly goes about writing letters and organising petitions.

"It never came naturally to me," she once told me. "In fact, in younger days I'd never say boo to a goose, however strongly I felt about something. Then one day I saw a quote of Martin Luther King's which looked as if it had been written just for me. He said, 'Our lives begin to end the day we become silent about things that matter.'

"So nowadays I speak up!"

Friday — October 14

YOU'VE planned a good deed? Well, do it today!
Why look for excuses to pause or delay?
For time quickly passes, the days will not wait,
Don't leave your good deed till it's all much too late.
The task, once you've started, you're sure to fulfil,
There's plenty of power in simple goodwill,
And when it's completed you know you'll feel grand,
So spring into action, and do what you've planned!

– Margaret Ingall.

After The Rain

Saturday — October 15

I'M sure you are familiar with the hymn "Lord Of The Dance". Yet when, in 1963, Sydney Carter wrote it, he was unsure of how it would be received. Would people understood what he meant? Would its non-traditional form be approved of? But as he explained, "I see Christ as the incarnation of the piper who is calling us. He dances that shape and pattern which is at the heart of our reality."

It can be a brave act to express our feelings without being confident of a positive reception. I'm quite certain I'm not the only one who was glad Sydney Carter had that courage.

Sunday — October 16

I SAW a beautiful photo of the Santa Maria della Pieta recently. It's a white octagonal church high in the Italian Appenine mountains. Beyond the 17th-century structure there was nothing but snowy peaks and the orange sunset. The photographer labelled the picture *The Lonely Church*.

It's a captivating – but slightly deceptive – image. You see, just behind the point where the photographer must have stood is a tenth century fortress, one of the main attractions in what is, after all, a National Park. So, perhaps the church isn't really so very lonely.

The image made me think of the times we might feel alone in our faith with the big, cold world ranged against us. Likewise, when we turn away from that daunting vista we inevitably find a great power and a strong refuge right behind us.

Monday — October 17

WE owe it to ourselves in this world of such seriousness to be a bit frivolous and light-hearted, if only for a day.

As the 18th-century English essayist, Charles Lamb, observed, "He who hath not a dram of folly in his mixture hath pounds of much worse matter in his composition." Life is too precious not to live it to its fullest.

Tuesday — October 18

WHEN I think of love," Mary told me, "I think of Mr Armstrong's woolly hat.

"His wife never really got the hang of knitting. The church knitting group were really encouraging. She ripped out that tea cosy so many times and never got it right. She was on the point of giving up the group. Then he told her to sew up the handle and spout holes and attach a woollen bobble. He wore it through that winter and the next, proclaiming his head had never been cosier.

"Mrs Armstrong kept attending the knitting group and made some of the best friends of her life, including me, because her husband wasn't too proud to wear a tea cosy on his head."

Wednesday — October 19

YOU know those annoying people who can find good in life even when their own situation is far from good? They are frustrating, I think, because secretly we wish we could be more like them. But how?

Well, at a time when his own fortunes were far from favourable the poet Lord Tennyson wrote –

"I see all things as they are. But through a kind of glory."

If we would be that kind of person we must learn to look for the glory.

Thursday — October 20

FRANK grew up in the same town as us but he left after secondary school and only returned many decades later.

"You know," he told Mary and me, "it turns out it wasn't the old town I was nostalgic for. It was my childhood I was missing."

"Pfft!" said Mary (who is a dear friend but not noted for her tact). "You should have kept it with you then."

Have you left your childhood somewhere along the way? It's not too late to run back and pick it up again.

Friday — October 21

SOME churches like to display witty or eye-catching messages on their noticeboards. But the one I saw outside a Methodist chapel recently was memorable not for any word-play, but for its simplicity.

It said, "Be ready for every good work. Speak evil of no-one. Avoid quarrels. Be gentle. Be kind."

Not great literature, you'll agree, and not designed for shock value or to promote a laugh. Just a simple way to change lives for the better – and bring the kingdom of Heaven that much closer to earth.

Saturday — October 22

HELEN was telling me about her mother who, although now well into her eighties, continues to write in the diaries that she's kept for nearly all her life.

"She can tell you what she was doing and what the weather was like for years past." Helen smiled. "But the thing I like best is the fact that every single day she makes a point of recording at least one positive thing that's happened."

I think that's an idea that we could all emulate. Even if we don't actually write it down, what an excellent thing to ponder on as we drift off to sleep. And what's more, I think it will be hard to confine ourselves to just one . . .

Sunday — October 23

I MUST say, David is the perfect walking companion," Linda said. "He warned me that I'd need my stoutest boots, but I was keen to try my new lightweight ones. They were soon in a horrible state, and what did David say then? Nothing. What a good friend he is!"

How easy it is to say, "I told you so" – and how unproductive. Which points to the truth of George Sala's remark that it can be hard "Not only to say the right thing in the right place but, far more difficult, to leave unsaid the wrong thing at the tempting moment."

And may we all be blessed with the knowledge of exactly when that is!

Monday — October 24

NEAR Haworth Village in Yorkshire's "Brontë Country" is a large rock outcrop known as Ponden Kirk. "Kirk", of course, means "church", but there is no explanation as to why the rock was so named. It's an imposing edifice, but it is not a place of worship . . .

But if you climb on to the top of the rock you get a truly breathtaking view of God's creation. Coming down again, you might remember that every place you ever stand is a worthy place to appreciate His handiwork and give thanks.

Tuesday — October 25

AGED twenty (back in 1726) Benjamin Franklin was determined to be a better man. So he drew up a list of virtues with the intention of practising them every day. The list included –

Think innocently and justly, and if you speak, speak accordingly
Forbear resenting injuries as much as you think they deserve.
Be not disturbed at trifles or accidents, common or unavoidable.
Speak only what will benefit others or yourself.
Wrong none.

Wednesday — October 26

HAVING just given his bike a thorough check-up, young Tony showed me his bicycle pump.

"There was a guy on a science programme," he said, "who invented a water filter that looked like this. It sucked up the muddiest liquid and pumped out water so pure that babies could drink it safely."

He lapsed into silence.

"I'd like my life to be like that," he eventually said. "Of course, the filter eventually clogged up. What I'd need would be something inside that actually changed the bad stuff I took in into the good stuff I gave back."

I left him to his contemplation. Walking on, I admired his ambition and considered that the best lives are often filters like that. The trick, as always, is to find that miraculous "something inside."

Thursday — October 27

A PHOTOGRAPH – or daguerreotype – taken of a French street in 1838 includes what is believed to be the oldest photographic image of a man. There were other people in the street, and horses pulling carts, but because the exposure was seven minutes long they passed through the image before it was captured. The man only shows up in it because he was having his shoes shined.

His place in history was made because he stuck around.

If you would make a mark in the history of someone's life there's no use wishing them the best as you fleetingly pass through. You have to stick around.

Friday — October 28

JOAN has always been a keen gardener, so when an accident left her in a wheelchair for several months, I was sure she must feel frustrated at not being able to carry out her usual spring and summer planting.

"You're right, Francis," she agreed. "Even though several good friends came to help, it wasn't the same. Then I discovered that there was something I could do all by myself." She laughed at my bemusement.

"I tried planting smiles," she told me, "just to see how many would come up. And it was amazingly successful. I found that every time I gave just one smile, I could generate loads. It was my best crop ever!"

In fact, now Joan may well have propagated even more than she realised – for if you are reading this with a smile, then that's another!

Saturday — October 29

A 16TH-CENTURY verse, written by a farmer to his son, tells us –
"Man does his best, God does the rest.

Man well intends, God the harvest sends."

The harvest has always been sent, and always will be. So we must hold up our half of the deal – and keep on doing our best.

Sunday — October 30

CREEDS have largely gone out of fashion these days. It used to be that knights, kings, even politicians, might have a stated set of beliefs that governed how they lived their lives.

Unfashionable or not, there is still much to be said for the idea.

Allow me, please, to share the creed of Howard Arnold Walter, a young man who died on missionary service in Sri Lanka in the early 20th century.

"I would be pure," he wrote, "for there are those who trust me;

I would be true, for there are those who care;

I would be strong, for there is much to suffer;

I would be brave, for there is much to dare;

I would be friend of all – the foe – the friendless;

I would be giving and forget the gift;

I would be humble, for I know my weakness;

I would look up – and laugh – and love and lift!"

Monday — October 31

EXCUSE the cooking smells!" Geraldine laughed when the Lady of the House and I called in to see her. "But I'm just in the middle of making some Friends Chutney."

Friends Chutney? With a name like that, we had to know more! So she told us how, a few years ago, when she and several friends realised that they'd all be making chutney from their various gluts of fruit or vegetables, they decided to share out the results.

That way they would not only get an assortment of varieties, they would also have the shared fun of trying out various flavours.

"In fact, it's been such a success," said Geraldine, "we now meet up regularly throughout the year."

A group bound together by chutney? But then I suspect almost anything can work out well if flavoured with a generous dollop of friendship!

November

Tuesday — November 1

THE very fine actor Jeremy Irons featured in two films concerned with time. He was the baddie in a version of H.G. Wells's "The Time Machine" and the narrator for the short film "The Chronoscope" (about a device for seeing into the past).

So it comes as no surprise to learn that he had his own, rather wonderful, take on time travel.

"We all have our time machines," he said. "Some take us back, they're called memories. Some take us forward, they're called dreams."

Wednesday — November 2

HAVE you noticed how many tests there are in the world?

This morning seemed to be full of them – first I bumped into young Ellie, who was not looking forward to her school spelling test. Then I saw Mary on her way to an eye test.

The paper I bought contained an article on the driving test and, returning home, I found the Lady of the House smiling over a magazine's personality test.

But of course, some of the tests we meet in life can be considerably more daunting. There are situations for which we can never revise or prepare, which do indeed test us to the limit.

If you happen to be facing such a trial, may I share with you these words of writer Doe Zantamata.

"It is only in our darkest hours that we may discover the true strength of the brilliant light within ourselves that can never, ever, be dimmed."

And that applies to you, just as it applies to each and every one of us. We are stronger than we know.

Just Five More Minutes!

Thursday — November 3

MEGHALAYA in northern India is considered to have the highest level of rainfall in the world. All that precipitation regularly floods streams and sweeps away bridges. So the locals grow tree roots from one bank to the other, intertwining them to create living bridges which can withstand the worst floods.

Such amazing feats take decades and are often done over two or three generations – but generations more will walk safely across those bridges.

We might never get to become bridge builders in that way, but in striving to pass on the best of the past, when it comes to love, wisdom and caring for the planet, to the next generation we, too, can become living bridges.

Friday — November 4

MOST of us prefer to keep our troubles to ourselves. After all, what possible good could come from sharing them around?

Or that was my thinking until I read these wise words by the actress and singer Dinah Shore. Ms Shore, who sang "Buttons And Bows" and "I Got It Bad (and that ain't good)" said, "Trouble is a part of your life and if you don't share it, you don't give the person who loves you a chance to love you enough."

After all, we would want them to give us the same chance!

Saturday — November 5

KEN showed me a video of a lepidopterist letting a butterfly out of a box. Children were gathered around for a good view but the butterfly took them by surprise, landing on a little boy's nose. He jumped and squealed but the butterfly hung on.

"It's like being loved," Ken said.

I couldn't understand the comparison, so he explained.

"It's beautiful, in your face, not always comfortable, a little scary – and such a blessed gift."

Sunday — November 6

THERE'S a scene in the film version of "Les Miserables" where Jean Valjean is arrested for stealing the Bishop's silverware. But, adding two ornate candlesticks to the haul, the Bishop persuades the gendarmes that the rest of the silverware was a gift from him.

The book, by Victor Hugo, adds a little back-story. The Bishop, a true man of God, has turned his palace into a hospital, sold his furniture to feed the poor, allocated most of his pay to charity and sold almost all his possessions. The silver candlesticks are the last expensive things he owns. But he has difficulty parting with them. Part of him wants to keep a little reminder of a richer life. But, for a thief's sake and for Christ's sake, he gives them away.

In doing so he frees Valjean – and also frees himself.

Monday — November 7

OH, to see the world through a child's eyes again!

She was about four years old and she was standing in a pile of leaves as deep as her wellingtons were tall.

"It's good fun playing in the dead leaves, isn't it?"

As I made my friendly suggestion a puzzled look crossed her face. Just then a stiff autumnal breeze lifted the leaves, filling the space between us with yellow, brown and red.

"They're not dead," she corrected me. "They're still dancing!"

Tuesday — November 8

THERE'S a story of a traveller who stopped by a farm to tell the farmer that his son was stuck in a mud hole.

"How deep's he in?" the farmer asked. On being told the boy was in up to his knees, the farmer lit his pipe and said, "Well, we've plenty of time to wait and see how it works out."

"I don't think so," the traveller said. "He's in head first!"

As with all things in life, there is a time to wait and see and a time to act. Wisdom knows the difference.

Wednesday — November 9

THE writer P.D. James probably had her tongue firmly in her cheek when she wrote, "It was one of those perfect English autumnal days which occur more frequently in memory than in life."

My own addition to that thought is that autumn isn't short of days worth visiting – even if only by standing at the back door or looking out through an open window.

Memories are fine, but the seasons and their changes include more perfect (or imperfect but wonderful in their own way) days than we can possibly remember. If only we don't forget to look.

Thursday — November 10

DO you know what I like about a spectacular sunset?" Harry asked. I looked around, confused. We were walking dogs on an evening where the clouds covered all the sky had to offer. I gave up.

"It's not its beauty for its own sake. It's the fact that most times the sun goes down unnoticed, but every once in a while . . ."

What Harry was saying was that just because many of our days are ordinary this doesn't take away the possibility that, every once in a while, we might be spectacular, too!

Friday — November 11

WHEN Marianne handed me a copy of her local parish magazine and told me it contained some beauty tips I might find interesting, I was surprised to say the least. But then I started reading:

"There is no lotion or potion on earth that enhances a face like a smile." Anon.

"Cheerfulness and contentment are great beautifiers and famous preservers of youthful looks." Charles Dickens.

"If you live close to God and His infinite grace,
You don't have to tell; it shows on your face." Anon.

Hmm. I think I shall start my new beauty regime right now!

Saturday — November 12

WELL," said Bill, "I have to take my hat off to my son, Simon. I thought he might give up college when he failed that exam. But no, he's decided that he'll stay on, work hard, and resit."

That excellent attitude epitomises some words of artist and author Mary Anne Radmacher who said, "Courage does not always roar. Sometimes it is a quiet voice at the end of the day saying: 'I will try again tomorrow'."

Good luck to you, Simon – and good luck to all of us who don't give up trying.

Sunday — November 13

I HAVE watched pigeons on bright days. The sunshine makes the feathers on their necks look first blue, then purple, then green. It makes for a beautiful effect as they fly away.

On a dull day the feathers are often simply grey. The wonderful effects come from their ability to reflect the sun.

You and I might be fairly ordinary on our own, but reflecting the Son we, too, can be wonderful and fly even higher.

Monday — November 14

IT can be strange how we humans perceive success. When James, after many triumphs travelling the world as a musician, finally decided to give up touring and return to his home town to teach, some folk told him it was a retrograde step.

Personally, I'm more of the opinion of author Terry Pratchett. In "A Hat Full of Sky", he writes: "Why do you go away? So that you can come back. So that you can see the place you came from with new eyes and extra colours. And the people there see you differently, too. Coming back to where you started is not the same as never leaving."

Sensible words. For after all, whether we are coming or going, it's good to remember that it's our own viewpoint that's really important.

Tuesday — November 15

*D*ON'T *forget your 'thank-you'!" my mother used to say,*
If asked for tea, or parties, or simply round to play.
"For kindness is a present, that often time outlives,
And simply saying 'thank-you' rewards the one who gives.

And now, as I grow older, I see her words were right
A thoughtful word or gesture can make a dark day bright,
So don't forget a 'thank-you', for though the words seem small,
You often will discover they're the biggest of them all!

– Margaret Ingall.

Wednesday — November 16

I **WAS** walking into town when Louisa passed me with a wave.

"I'm just off to visit my great-uncle Peter," she told me. "It's his ninetieth birthday today, so to celebrate we're going to visit a preserved railway for a trip down the line." She grinned. "Although as far as he's concerned, it's always full steam ahead!"

I knew what she meant, for I have met Louisa's great-uncle, and never fail to be impressed by his liveliness and vitality. But as Samuel Ullman once pointed out, "Nobody grows old merely by living a number of years. We grow old by deserting our ideals. Years may wrinkle the skin, but to give up enthusiasm wrinkles the soul."

May Great-uncle Peter – and indeed all of us – stay for ever unwrinkled!

Thursday — November 17

W**INTER**! Dark, bleak, wet. What good is it to anyone?

The poet Dame Edith Sitwell described the season as "The time for comfort, for good food and warmth, for the touch of a friendly hand and for a talk beside the fire: it is the time for home."

Of course, we can do all of those things at any time of the year. But aren't they all the more special when the wind is howling outside?

Friday — November 18

THE actress Marion Cotillard was talking about the process of making a movie recently.

"I found it very interesting to allow myself to be lost, because I knew that I had this amazing guide . . . You abandon yourself for a story and a director that will make it all work."

Does that sound like life, anyone?

Saturday — November 19

MILITARY ceremonial epaulettes, worn on the shoulders of uniforms, can denote regiment, rank or an honour bestowed. Sometimes they have more tassels than a hand-woven rug. But a naturalist and philosopher was proud to recall wearing a different kind.

"I once had a sparrow alight upon my shoulder while I was hoeing in a village garden," he wrote, "and I felt that I was more distinguished by that circumstance than I should have been by any epaulette I could have worn."

After all, what greater honour could nature bestow than that a bird – one of the most timid forms of creature – sees you as a safe place to rest?

Sunday — November 20

THERE can be few things more awe-inspiring – and more difficult to reproduce – than a sunset in all its glory. Painters and photographers have tried with varying degrees of success.

But the Scottish preacher and writer George MacDonald took another approach. He wanted to inspire a similar feeling in people by loving them and showing them how cherished they were by the One who created the sun and the sky, the night and the day.

"If I can put one touch of rosy sunset into the life of any man or woman," he wrote, "I shall feel that I have worked with God."

What more beautiful work could there be?

Monday — November 21

TITHING is usually taken as giving money to the church but Alexander Nowell had a different way of looking at it. He was Dean of St Paul's in the 16th century – and a keen angler. He called the hours spent on the riverbank a tithe of his time. Then, after spending ten percent of his day fishing, he gave his catch to the poor.

Did he spend that time in contemplation of God? Who knows? But he must have been appreciating the wonders of Creation.

The poor who lived between the fishing-hole and St Paul's definitely benefited from Doctor Nowell's time-out. Imagine the good we could do if we all gave God that kind of tithe. And if we can make a relaxing hobby out of it, so much the better!

Tuesday — November 22

COMMUNITIES based around specific ways of life often have phrases unique to them. I read that German miners used to greet each other with the words "Glück auf".

After the initial seam of coal (or gold or copper) was worked out the miners would dig on in hope of finding another. "Glück auf" is a shortened version of a phrase that means, "I hope another lode opens up for you."

Many of us go through life hoping and trusting that our path will lead to something worthwhile. And in that spirit may I borrow the old greeting and wish you a heartfelt "Glück auf!"

Wednesday — November 23

THE 17th-century poet John Dryden listed four character traits he thought of as "the bread of mankind and the staff of life."

Surely attributes of such importance would be complex and difficult to achieve! Not at all. They are affability, mildness, tenderness and good nature.

We often make life more complicated than it needs to be but as Dryden shows us it is, in essence, beautifully simple!

Deepest Blue

Thursday — November 24

ALL too often American phrases, spellings and traditions creep into British life.

One tradition that hasn't yet crossed the Atlantic (although we hear more and more about it) is Thanksgiving Day. But perhaps that is a tradition we might benefit from taking on board – if we took the advice of writer and editor Edward Sandford Martin.

Writing in the early years of the 20th century, he opined, "Thanksgiving Day comes, by statute, once a year but to the honest man it comes as frequently as the heart of gratitude will allow."

Let's find a reason to give thanks every day.

Friday — November 25

NOW – who likes facing problems?
Not many, I suspect,
Yet whether large or tiny,
They all have this effect:
Each problem we encounter,
And yes, each failure, too,
Will always make us stronger,
Just try – you'll find it's true!

– Margaret Ingall.

Saturday — November 26

THE old wisdom suggests you can light a thousand candles from one candle and the life of that candle will not be shortened.

I was thinking about that. Each time a new candle is lit, a little of the energy consuming the original candle is transferred away. So, if anything, lighting all those other candles might help the original last longer. Very philosophical, I know!

So, would our lives be shortened or lengthened if we spent all our energies "lighting candles" by lifting other people up? I don't know.

But I do know we would spend it surrounded by a lot more happy people.

Sunday — November 27

GARY was adopted when he was eight. I've known him and his adoptive family for years.

So, I was surprised when he introduced me to a lady I'd never met before and said, "Francis, this is my mum."

After the church service, I saw her standing alone for a moment, wiping away a tear.

"I didn't expect it to be like this," she explained. "Gary has introduced me to everyone here and every time he said, 'This is my mum' I heard nothing but pride.

"No recrimination because I gave him up. No anger at me hardly having been involved in his life."

She felt she didn't deserve it, but Gary wasn't going to let that stop him. He's a man of faith and I'm sure he knew God would be glad he and his mother were together.

And I could just imagine God looking down, smiling, and saying, "This is my child!"

Monday — November 28

THE students were discussing which famous person had inspired them most.

"Mother Teresa," Lucy declared. "She did so much to help the poor and destitute."

"Nelson Mandela," said Will. "He didn't just win the battle against apartheid, he was forgiving towards his enemies afterwards."

"But what about Florence Nightingale?" Rose offered. "Think how hard it must have been to walk away from a comfortable life, and into all the horrors of the Crimean War."

They turned to Toby, who had yet to contribute.

"Well," he said hesitantly, "they're all to be much admired, but I think I take my inspiration from those around me. If we just look and listen, there are so many ordinary people with their own quiet stories of courage and perseverance – I just hope I can be like that, too."

Well said! Unsung heroes they may be – but heroes all the same.

Tuesday — November 29

I KNEW she would do it!

As I walked along the path with Mary I just knew she would have to kick up the piles of rust-coloured leaves. When she finished, she looked up at the trees that overhung the fence; the trees that had given her that moment of childish pleasure.

"You know," she said thoughtfully, "they do that every year. But it never makes any one of them less of a tree, shedding all those old leaves. In fact, it lets them grow stronger the coming spring. Now, if only we could let last year's problems blow away in the wind without thinking it diminished us."

It brought to mind something I ought to have let go. Then, in the spirit of new growth, I raced Mary to the next pile of leaves!

Wednesday — November 30

THE year is fading quickly, Lord,
A new one lies ahead,
And only You know what's in store
Along the path we tread.
There could be days of happiness,
Of laughing in the sun,
Of great achievement and success,
New projects just begun.

There may be shadows on our path
With days of tears and pain,
With times when we must seek new hope
And rainbows after rain.
We know the trees will bud again,
We know the birds will sing,
We know that winter passes by
And we will welcome spring.

And so as all the seasons change
Lord, help our spirits climb,
And let us share in love and joy
The precious gift of time.

– Iris Hesselden.

December

"A RE we nearly there yet?"
Yes, I'm quite sure that question will bring a groan of recognition from anyone who has ever travelled with a small child on a long journey! And yet it's natural as a child to be impatient, for it is only as we grow older that we learn that we can't always have what we want right now.

Or do we? All right, I must admit that I, too, am liable to get fretful if I'm hoping for a speedy outcome in a situation over which I have little or no control.

At moments like those, I try to dwell on a thought from Elisabeth Elliot who reminded us: "Restlessness and impatience change nothing except our peace and joy. Peace does not dwell in outward things, but in the heart prepared to wait trustfully and quietly on Him who has all things safely in His hands."

The perfect reassurance that whatever time we get there, it will certainly be the right time.

F EW of us sail through life without meeting any kind of obstacle, but John seemed to be managing it well until, as a keen sportsman, he was signed on as professional rugby player.

Only days afterwards, he suffered a badly broken leg which threatened to end his career before it had begun.

"Happily, the enforced rest gave me time to discover an American writer called T.F. Hodge," he said. "He's had a varied career, including being an athlete and coach, so I guess he knows what he's talking about.

"Now, every morning I wake up I repeat his words to myself: 'Head up, heart open. To better days!'"

Only seven short words – but what an abundance of good advice!

Saturday — December 3

STACEY never used to bother sending Christmas cards to her neighbours. After all, she didn't know them all that well and it seemed just a touch hypocritical – not to mention the added expense!

But, year after year, in spite of this, her neighbours kept sending her cards with friendly, festive messages. And the longer she didn't send out cards, the more she found herself appreciating the fact that the cards kept coming, and the warm wishes that came along with them.

So, this year, as a thank you, she sent cards to everyone in the street!

It reminded me of the Edwin Markham verse.

"He drew a circle that shut me out – Heretic, rebel, a thing to flout. But love and I had the wit to win: We drew a circle and took him in!"

Stacey's neighbours drew a loving circle, and kept drawing it. And eventually my young friend joined them inside it!

Sunday — December 4

THE 19th-century Cornish preacher Billy Bray experienced a life of opposites. His own father died when he was young, but he became father to two orphans as well as his own children.

A riotous singer during years of drunkenness, his church services after he came to God were noted for the spontaneous songs of praise.

He once told a story of a farmer whose barn-top weather vane was inscribed with the words *God Is Love*.

A sceptic asked Rev. Bray, "Does that mean God's love is as changeable as the weather?"

"No," he replied. "It means that God loves you no matter which way the wind blows."

Like Billy Bray, those of us who have ups and downs in our lives will know the beauty of that idea.

Monday — December 5

I DO enjoy reading the words of learned men from the past (and they do tend to be men), but I did smile when I read this comment by Mary Ward, a 19th-century British lady of letters.

"It had begun to be recognised with a great burst of astonishment that, after all (John Stuart) Mill and Herbert Spencer had not said the last word on all things in heaven and earth."

As educated and wise as those gentlemen (and Mrs Ward) were, I am very glad we still have some great and beautiful thoughts to find for ourselves!

Tuesday — December 6

I N the run-up to Christmas it's not too unusual to see folk scurrying round with lists, but Jean's was rather different.

"I came across this in a book," she explained as she showed me. "It's not exactly a conventional gift list, but I liked it so much I copied it down. What do you think of it, Francis?"

To those who have hurt you – forgiveness

To those who try your patience – tolerance.

To a friend – your heart.

To all men – charity.

To a child – a good example.

To yourself – respect.

Now, that's something worth remembering, even without a list!

Wednesday — December 7

I HAD to laugh when I read of the schooldays of the 19th-century children's writer Sarah Parton. Her headmistress described her as "the worst behaved pupil" but "the one I loved the most."

Contradictory? Yes. But that ability to be marvellously contradictory – naughty but lovable; disapproving but adoring – is surely one of the most charming traits human beings possess.

Thursday — December 8

A **FRIENDSHIP** *needs building, so craft it with care,*
Start some foundations with interests you share.
Stack the walls firmly with bricks made of trust,
Give time to settle, develop, adjust.

A roof will be wanted, so fix with goodwill,
Though storms may occur it will shelter you still.
Put in some windows and polish them bright,
You need to view all in a positive light.

A generous hearth with a steady warm flame
Burns away squabbles, or coolness or blame,
Such methods build friendships enduring and strong,
Rewarding, fulfilling to last a life long.

– Margaret Ingall.

Friday — December 9

W**HEN** I started thinking about what to do next, I found I was almost paralysed by uncertainty."

I overheard that remark while walking down the street so, tantalisingly, I never did hear the full story – but I could certainly sympathise.

Sometimes life can throw up such difficult choices that it almost takes away our ability to make decisions.

Happily, we eventually muddle through, but the saddest scenario of all is to be so worried about getting it wrong that we choose to live life entirely safely, avoiding ever trying to stretch ourselves for fear of failure.

I like the quotation of George Bernard Shaw, who pronounced: "A life spent making mistakes is not only more honourable, but more useful than a life spent doing nothing."

I particularly like his use of the word "honourable" – and next time I make a mistake, I'm sure I will be glad to remind myself of it!

Saturday — December 10

WOULD it surprise you if I were to suggest you might easily become one of the world's great thinkers?

No, you don't have to study philosophy or learn abstract mathematics or become a computer genius, but you might still be able to elevate your thinking to a higher level.

The great writer and philosopher G.K. Chesterton once declared, "Thanks are the highest form of thought."

So, cultivate a habit of gratitude and you can tell your friends you are thinking with the greats!

Sunday — December 11

ANTONY, a second-century monk, had one ambition – to make the most of God's gift: to be better at this thing called life!

Therefore he visited much, was a courteous and considerate guest, and sought out only the best in the people he met.

He learned patience from one, gentleness from another, loyalty from a third . . . and so on. Along the way he became known as "God's friend."

I imagine if someone knocked on my door, or yours, looking to learn from our best qualities, we might come to call them friend as well – after we got over the shock of someone thinking we were worth learning from!

Monday — December 12

RELIGIOUS sceptics say that Christianity is nothing more than a crutch. However, believers have a personal relationship with God, a relationship born of faith in Jesus, which is about strength and trust, whatever the situation.

"We are troubled on every side, yet not distressed. We are perplexed but not in despair."

Consider this reading from 2 Corinthians 4 today – and have faith.

Tuesday — December 13

IN the 1935 film "Enchanted April", two ladies discuss which of them was the first to meet a certain gentleman.

"I met him at the end of the path," said one.

"But I met him at the hearth-side," said the other, "which is surely the real end of the path."

I liked the idea that all paths should end at a homely hearth, but it also made me think of the One who is really worth meeting in this life. We might expect to find Him at any point on the journey. And having found Him once, we need to keep walking with Him until we can both sit together at the Heavenly hearth. Because Heaven must surely have a fireplace!

Wednesday — December 14

NOT much is known of Andres de Andrada, except that he lived in Spain and Mexico in the 17th century. That his life knew good times and bad, and that he eventually found happiness, is evident from the poetry he left behind, including lines as relevant now as they were in the days of the Spanish empire.

"Poor is the man that roves o'er lands and seas
In chase of treasures that soon cease to please.
Me smaller things suffice,
A simple seat 'midst my loved ones in some green retreat,
A book, a friend, and slumbers that declare
A tranquil bliss and vacancy from care."

Thursday — December 15

THE inventor of the telephone, Alexander Graham Bell, was a student at Edinburgh University. On a page of a recent calendar for alumni, this quote from Bell was printed: "When one door closes, another door opens. But we often look so long and regretfully upon the closed one that we do not see the ones which open for us."

As this year draws to a close, consider this a resolution and look for opportunities.

Friday — December 16

THE Cratchit family's Christmas dinner, in Dickens's "A Christmas Carol", was an impoverished affair. But they took great delight in every aspect of it. When Bob Cratchit pours a hot drink for a toast he pours it into "two tumblers and a custard cup without a handle."

In describing the humble drinking vessels the author suggests that they served "as well as golden goblets would have done."

What raised a poor meal to a Christmas feast; a custard cup to the standard of a golden goblet? The best gift anyone can have at Christmas. The love of a family.

Saturday — December 17

THERE'S a festival in Peru called Takanakuy. It's a day set aside for settling grievances, which is done by boxing. But after the bouts are over the celebrations continue and the slates are wiped clean. Grudges and enmities are left behind.

Now, if only we could have a day like that – but without the fighting!

Well, we do. Takanakuy takes place each December 25, the same day we set aside for peace on earth and goodwill to all men. Perhaps this year we can extend that goodwill beyond Christmas Day, leaving old disputes behind, and making a New Year of new beginnings.

Sunday — December 18

THE much-loved comedian Bob Hope was once asked how he thought "modern" Christmases compared with traditional ones.

"My idea of Christmas, whether old-fashioned or modern, is very simple," he replied. "It's loving others. Come to think of it, why do we have to wait for Christmas to do that?"

Perhaps the celebration is the reminder we often need of what's important; love from on high, to be shared with every one of us.

And if we carry that spirit forward, then there's "Hope" for the New Year – and every year!

Plenty For All!

Monday — December 19

I WONDER if you have ever heard of Amy Carmichael?

Born in Ireland in 1867, she grew up to become one of the most respected missionaries of her time.

With an unwavering trust in her calling, she eventually ended up in India where, despite fever and ill health, she remained for years, channelling her considerable practical energies into saving numerous children from lives of poverty and desperation, finally founding the Dohnavur Fellowship to carry on the work.

At times it must have seemed overwhelming. But did she falter? No.

As she herself expressed it: "God is the God of the waves and billows, and they are still His when they come over us. Again and again we have proved that the overwhelming thing does not overwhelm . . . We were cast down, but not destroyed."

Brave words from a remarkable woman.

Tuesday — December 20

WHEN I was little," Jim was telling me one day not long ago, "I had a best friend who was always rather boastful about his uncle who worked as a teacher in some of the very poorest parts of the world.

"My friend never stopped going on about all the good things his uncle had done, and how amazing he was, until I reached the point where I decided this uncle must be the most boring person in the world."

"And did you ever find out if you were right?" I asked him with a grin.

"I did," Jim replied. "He once came home for a visit, and I found out for myself what a great man he actually was.

"Since then," Jim went on, "I've had to agree with what C.S. Lewis once said: 'How little people know, who think that holiness is dull. When one meets the real thing, it's irresistible!'"

Well, C.S. Lewis always was a wise old owl.

Wednesday — December 21

OUR young friend was delighted with her new home and we were pleased to pay her a visit.

In pride of place on the handsome fireplace was a small plaque she had bought in Canada and brought home carefully wrapped and packed.

The words seemed really appropriate for her and perhaps for us all at some time in our lives.

"Sometimes you just have to take the leap and build your wings on the way down."

Now and then we all need a leap of faith plus a helping of hope and courage!

Another of her new purchases was a purple door mat with the words *Carpe Diem*.

Yet again, words to encourage: "Seize the day" is something we must all learn to do.

I hope we can follow her example and build our wings whenever they are needed!

Thursday — December 22

THERE can be fewer more wonderful examples of this than a kindness supposedly done by Bishop Nicholas of Myra.

A man in his town had three daughters who were engaged to be married. But they all needed a dowry. Either this man would break himself financially, or he would break his daughters' hearts.

Somehow Nicholas got into their house where the daughters' stockings were hanging up to dry. Then he dropped three bags of gold coins into the stockings.

A kind act, to be sure, but he couldn't have foreseen that millions of children would get bulging Christmas stockings for years after because of it!

Could you inspire something so wonderful? I'm sure good old Saint Nick didn't think he could. But you never know!

Friday — December 23

So long ago, so long ago, the story first began,
Of how, upon a winter's night, our Lord was born as Man.
Yet though we know the tale so well, we still draw close to hear
Those old familiar details which remain so fresh, so dear.

The star that rose in eastern skies, and lit the desert sands,
The journey of the three wise men who came from distant lands,
Poor shepherds in their lonely fields, who watched their flock by
* night,*
And angel hosts whose heavenly joy transformed the dark to light.

The sleeping town of Bethlehem, the humble inn nearby,
The stable where the midnight hush was cut by newborn's cry
And there within, in lantern light, amidst the dust and straw,
A mother looked upon her child with love and hope and awe.

Oh, may this tale for ever fill each listening heart with cheer,
And may it never cease to bring new hope to all who hear,
And let it live throughout the years, and never stay untold
To fill our hearts with wonderment till even Time grows old.

– Margaret Ingall.

Saturday — December 24

CHRISTMAS is for children.

There, I've said it! But before you think I am being too "Bah, humbug" like Ebenezer Scrooge, I would point out that I know children of all ages.

But, still, what is there in it for those of us just a little past the excitement of listening for reindeer hooves on the rooftop?

Charles Dickens, the creator of Ebenezer Scrooge, believed it offered gifts less tangible than before, but perhaps more wonderful.

"Happy, Happy Christmas," he wrote, "that can win us back to the delusions of our childhood days, recall to the old man the pleasures of his youth, and transport the traveller back to his own fireside and quiet home!"

Sunday — December 25

TODAY it's Christmas Day. It's a time when we can sometimes be left wondering if all the expense, trouble and stress was worth it!

Well, while you are celebrating this religious feast, consider these words spoken by American humourist Erma Bombeck:

"There's nothing sadder in this world than to wake on Christmas morning and not be a child."

May the child in you re-emerge this special day.

Monday — December 26

NOW that the festivities and the hustle and bustle of Christmas are over for another year, many of us find ourselves feeling a little flat and perhaps even a bit down now that there is nothing left to look forward to.

But as we approach the end of the year and winter begins to wane, we find that the days are growing longer and green buds start to appear.

We see the sun beginning to appear more often. We see the tiny snowdrops bravely start to raise their heads above the frozen ground, and all of a sudden we begin to feel more hopeful and cheerful.

For this time of year, I have always felt that this prayer by Edward Hayes is worth knowing and repeating.

I hope you agree.

"O God, my Father, Creator of the sun which makes the seasons, I rejoice in the gift of ever-growing light. With joyfulness I greet this new spring that rises from a grey winter of long nights.

"Great and generous are You, my God, who has given us the rich variety of ever-changing seasons.

"For this I thank You."

Perhaps we all need to take time to say thank you to God for bringing us through the winter – and an especial, heartfelt thank you for the precious hope of spring.

Tuesday — December 27

THE Lady of the House was smiling when she returned from a visit to the local garden centre.

"I bumped into Mary," she told me, "so we decided to share a pot of tea in the cafe. But as she poured it out she was so engrossed in telling me about her planned new rose bushes that she forgot to stop! Fortunately no damage was done, but it did remind me of what Jim Stovall said: 'In times when we yearn to have more in our lives, we should dwell on the things we already have. In doing so, we will often find that our lives are already full to overflowing.'"

Very true – but in Mary's case it looks as if her life really is coming up roses!

Wednesday — December 28

TOMMY was doing his homework, dictionary by his side.

"I was about to look up the meaning of the word 'procrastinate'." He grinned. "But then I decided to leave it till later."

Unfortunately, a lot of us are all too familiar with that instinctive urge to put off anything we're not quite sure about. Which is why I also appreciate a quote from writer Paulo Coelho: "When we least expect it, life sets us a challenge to test our courage and willingness to change; at such a moment, there is no point in pretending that nothing has happened or in saying that we are not yet ready. The challenge will not wait."

Next time things in my life need to change, I shall set about it straight away. And they might even turn out to be for the better!

Thursday — December 29

OUR local parish lay preacher was giving a sermon last Sunday in the absence of the usual minister. One quote from his words stood out, namely: "Our desire to please God is our highest driving force for obeying God."

A thought-provoking observation, I'm sure you'll agree.

Friday — December 30

YOU'D like to see my garden?
You may – but nothing's there,
For all's so dull and dreary
This dismal time of year.
So please excuse its bleakness –
But wait, what's that you see . . .?
A little clump of snowdrops?
Green buds upon that tree?
But nothing else worth seeing;
Oh, how this winter grieves . . .
But something else you've noticed?
Green shoots beneath dead leaves?
And yellow stars of jasmine?
And pussy willows, too?
Some cyclamens half hidden,
Yet growing straight and true?

I'm glad you came a-calling,
And noticed every nook,
Yes, life is full of wonders –
We only have to look!

– Margaret Ingall.

Saturday — December 31

MOST of us call it New Year's Eve and the celebrations usually begin in the run-up to midnight. But Gracie calls it Jar Day and her celebrations start shortly after she wakes up.

I had to ask – and she was only too happy to explain. A few years ago, she was gifted a glass jar of sweets. Watching her waistline, she shared the sweets out amongst the family. But she kept the jar. Then, every time a positive, happy, wonderful thing happened in her life she wrote a note about it and saved it in the jar.

All throughout Jar Day she reads the notes and reminds herself how much fun there was in the previous 364 days.

What better way to make sure New Year's Day is one of happy anticipation?

PHOTOGRAPH LOCATIONS:

Heavenly Heights – Radcliffe Camera, Oxford.
Safe Harbour – Portland Bill Lighthouse, Dorset.
Still Waters – Sennen Cove, West Cornwall.
Tumbling Down – Isle of Skye.
A Fine Day Out! – Cambuskenneth Abbey, Stirling.
Beautiful Borders – Abbotsford House, Galashiels.
Rugged Landscape – Loch Maree, Wester Ross.
Golden Glory – Avenue Gardens, Regent's Park, London.
Pretty Patterns – Pitmedden Garden, Aberdeenshire.
In Dublin's Fair City – Samuel Beckett Bridge, Dublin.
Suspended In Time – Carrick-A-Rede Rope Bridge, Co. Antrim.
Island Sanctuary – Iona Abbey, Iona.
After The Rain – Aber Falls, Gwynedd.
Deepest Blue – Mullion Cove Harbour, Cornwall.
Winter In The City – Edinburgh.

ACKNOWLEDGEMENTS:

A Fine Day Out! – I. Robertson.
Beautiful Borders – Tom Parker.
Pretty Patterns – Willie Shand.

All other images Thinkstockphotos.